PRENUP PARTNERSHIP
A Guide To Getting A Prenup You Both Love

eBook ASIN: B0CHBJ7BYR
Paperback ISBN: 9798339259251
Hardcover: 979-8-303-92509-0
Expanded Distribution: 979-8-218-56955-6

Cover design by Sooraj Mathew

**The ArtCat**
CREATIVE SERVICES

Edited by Hilary Jastram | www.bookmarkpub.com

**Bookmark**
PUBLISHING HOUSE

# PRENUP
# PARTNERSHIP

## Protect Your Money
## And Your Relationship

### *A GUIDE TO GETTING A*
### *PRENUP YOU BOTH LOVE*

**KAYLIN DILLON** CFP®

# DEDICATION

---

*To Grayson, for holding the torch while I scribbled in the dark.*
*Here's to getting more right than wrong.*

*I love you.*

# GET IN TOUCH

For Financial Planning: www.kdfp.co

For Prenup Resources: www.prenupcoach.com

# EARLY PRAISE FOR PRENUP PARTNERSHIP

*"If you've ever wondered 'Should I get a prenup?' This is the book for you. Kaylin walks you through this important decision with empathy and tactical advice.*
*"You'll walk away with clarity about the best path forward and a wealth of resources to deepen your relationship with your partner. That's priceless."*
**—Beth Williams, Founder & Lead Financial Planner,**
***Future Wallet***

*"Everything inheritors, business owners, real estate investors, and their partners need to know about prenups!*
*"Kaylin has essential advice to help couples openly and honestly communicate their financial needs through the prenup process. Her guidance, education, and case studies will help couples navigate getting a prenup and strengthen their relationship in the process."*
**—Katherine Fox, CFP®, Founder & Advisor for Inheritors, *Sunnybranch Wealth***

*"Kaylin is incredibly gifted in both knowledge and presentation of prenups. She is able to tackle important nuances of this tricky subject and has dramatically shifted my approach to the conversation."*
**—Nathan Astle, Licensed Marriage and Family Therapist, CFT - I™,**
***Financial Therapy Clinical Institute***

*"Prenuptial agreements have an intimidating stigma. However, Kaylin guided us through the process with grace, understanding, and expertise. Because of Kaylin and her work with us on our prenuptial agreement, my husband and I now have a marriage based on the trust that we are together for the right reasons. We can never thank her enough for her role in laying down the foundation of our new life together stronger than we thought possible."*
**—Brooke Elliott-Lowry**

*"Kaylin was very knowledgeable and able to address all of our questions related to prenuptial agreements, potential clauses, alimony, etc. It helped us better understand what options were best for our situations. I really appreciated that the session included an organized checklist of steps to include/ consider when drafting a prenuptial agreement. I would recommend her services to anyone interested in learning more."*
**—Alvonee C. Penn**

# TABLE OF CONTENTS

# A LOVE LETTER TO MY PRENUP-GETTING COUPLES

---

*While most pretend they don't think about it,*
*You think it, and you say it.*

*Creating safety for your partner matters to you.*
*You don't apologize for wanting safety for yourself, too.*

*As much as you value clear boundaries,*
*You place your relationship higher.*

*But most of all, dear couples,*
*You look the legal contract that is marriage straight*
*in the eye and say,*

*"We're doing this on our terms."*

# INTRODUCTION

YOU MAY HAVE YOUR OWN IDEAS about what a prenuptial agreement is based on popular culture, celebrity tabloids, your religion, or friends and family. Perhaps you've had your own experience with a prenup. There are plenty of stories out there of bad prenup experiences. I've also been a part of many good ones.

I am not going to focus on the sensationalist stories. Instead, I am here to give you the truth. And the truth is many people do not understand everything a prenup governs. They don't get that it is about so much more than a document put into play after a marriage. A prenup done well should actually *protect the marriage.*

I wrote this book to help you find a better way to use this legal tool, the prenup. Before you go any further, I invite you to hold some space for this new impression of what a prenup is. If you're reading this book with a negative view of prenups, I urge you to open up to come away with a more neutral view of them. When used correctly, they can help you, not hurt you.

Of course, how you go about getting a prenup and what you include in one matter, and we will talk about that, I promise. But I don't want to get ahead of myself.

First, let's begin with what a prenup actually is.

## WHAT IS A PRENUPTIAL AGREEMENT?

A prenuptial agreement is a contract between two partners that takes effect upon marriage. It's sometimes called a premarital agreement or an antenuptial agreement and is usually written to supersede the default state laws governing marital property. Put more simply, a prenup usually spells out how a couple's assets will be divided if the couple gets divorced.

But . . . that's just one use of this contract.

Here's what you might not expect: prenups aren't limited to divorce terms. A prenup can also be used to govern estate terms (instead of a will or trust) or to set rules that apply *during* your marriage. It can actually make your couplehood stronger. We'll get into those details later.

I started my practice with the intention of doing financial planning for people who, like me, already have a prenuptial agreement and want help managing separate assets while also planning together. (I see so many financial advisors out there who aren't comfortable doing joint planning for couples with separate assets, so I knew this was an area where more resources were needed.)

Once my business was up and running, it didn't take long before I started getting inquiries from engaged couples considering a prenuptial agreement. Email after email came in, asking, "Do I need a prenup?" "How do I bring it up to my partner?" and "Do I really just call up an attorney and get started?" I hadn't planned for these specific questions, but one distinctive need came through loud and clear: Couples want help bridging the gap between "Do I need a prenup?" and actually getting one.

The more traditional reasons for getting a prenup in the past (big wealth or family business interests) didn't really call for a pleasant prenup-getting experience. You either needed one or you didn't, and you could either suck it up or not.

Now, couples are eager for a more attractive option, and happily, that does exist. Everything you need to know about that better route is in this guidebook, which is why I wrote it. You need to know about it, just as you need misinformation about prenups debunked.

In my research and through working with clients, I believe that the majority of couples aren't opting for a prenup largely due to misconceptions. *Newsweek* reports in a 2022 Harris Poll that 15% of US adults have a prenup, while 35% of unmarried individuals today say they'd sign one.[1]

It doesn't surprise me that couples want a better process for this important legal document. After working with a few engaged couples on their financial plans and helping them prepare for a prenup, I realized the best practices for getting a prenup really aren't common knowledge. Not even among professionals. That's when I formalized my process for engaged couples. Hence, my prenup coaching service was born.

# WHAT IS A PRENUP COACH?

A prenup coach guides and supports couples through the process of preparing for and getting a prenuptial agreement. It's advantageous because an attorney can only represent one partner during this process. Working with a prenup coach ensures you have a guide who can support both of you as needed.

Attorneys are also expensive and are generally not in the business of helping with the preparation part of the process, which I will cover in a later section of the book. When you apply what I am sharing in these pages, by the time you reach your attorney, they'll be ready to start the first draft. Consider your prenup coach a part

---

1   Suzanne Blake, "Prenups Aren't Just for the Wealthy Anymore," Newsweek, October 27, 2023, https://www.newsweek.com/more-americans-are-signing-prenups-1838768.

of the team, who will help you with your attorney search and keep you looped in through every stage of the process, so you won't feel blindsided (as can sometimes be the case).

I built my coaching business to be intuitive based on my own experience and what I wanted throughout the various steps of creating my now-husband's and my prenup. In 2009, without knowing any better yet, I created a prenup the traditional way. Despite thinking I was on the same page as my partner, I soon found out I wasn't, and what followed was highly stressful for both of us. I don't want you to learn the hard way. So, here's a quick description of the traditional way (aka the wrong way) to get a prenup.

# THE WRONG WAY TO GET A PRENUP

- **Step 1:** Partner A requests a prenup from their attorney.
- **Step 2:** Attorney A drafts the most protective prenup possible under the law. (It's the attorney's job to have Partner A's best interests in mind, after all.)
- **Step 3:** Attorney B shares this document with Partner B and says something to the effect of, "No way are you signing this." (It's their job, after all, to advocate for Partner B's best interests.)
- **Step 4:** Through confusion and hurt feelings, Partner A and Partner B go back and forth, largely through their attorneys, until they finally land on an agreement.

It requires no imagination to picture how miserable this approach is, not to mention, expensive. Unfortunately, it's still too common. Well-meaning advisors suggest prenups as a course of business. Wealth advisors often say, "Just keep the emotions out of it, and get it done." This type of advice ignores the reality that money is inherently an emotional topic.

In her book *Engaged Healthy, Wealthy, and Wise*, Coventry Edwards-Pitt interviewed wealth inheritors and their significant others about what it was like to merge their lives, particularly with respect to managing finances. One of her findings was that when family members or outside advisors instruct a couple to get a prenup, the process tends to be traumatic for the couple. Her primary takeaway was that prenups are best avoided if possible. What's interesting is that her findings only reinforce my perception—prenups can be a productive tool for a couple *when they agree on the decision to get one.*

I'll share a quote from the book, which I like to use as an eye-opener. Edwards-Pitt proves my point about ensuring you are both seeing eye to eye with healthy money conversations when she says, "In many cases, they (prenups) are the suggestion of a diligent wealth advisor or estate attorney attempting to mitigate risk—which, unfortunately, is defined too narrowly by the wealth advising industry as money lost rather than human relationships damaged."

I read it as: "If you want a prenup as a matter of risk mitigation, keep in mind that tending to your emotional connection with your partner is also a matter of risk mitigation."

I can't tell you how many calls I've received from distressed brides who've just been handed a first draft of a prenup. They're overwhelmed and offended. (I suspect this is happening to men, too, but for one reason or another, they aren't the ones calling me in a last-ditch effort to save their prenup negotiations.)

*This litigious approach to getting a prenup begs one very important question: Is it in your best interest to win a premarital negotiation, or is it in your best interest to set a healthy foundation for a happy marriage?*

The good news is that you can get a prenup while building that healthy foundation. I've taken many couples through the process of preparing for their prenup, and every one of them has had a positive experience.

Did they avoid uncomfortable conversations? No.

Did they see eye-to-eye on every point? No.

But if you explore getting a prenuptial agreement with care for your relationship and as a joint project, your relationship wins every time. Couples tell me they have deeper trust and more confidence in their future together after working through this process that I'm going to share with you.

Estate planning attorney and author of nine books on prenups and estate planning, L. Paul Hood, Jr., allowed me to interview him for this book and notes, "If couples would have a discussion before they got married, in a healthy, nurturing environment, with people who are shepherding them through that process, we would all be better off."

You'll notice I don't jump straight into the pros and cons of pre-nuptial agreements in this book, but that's here, too.

First, I will teach you how to talk to your partner about money and plan how you want to manage your finances during marriage. This way, by the time you have learned about the pros and cons of prenups, you'll be ready to consider whether one is right for both of you—you'll have the tools to make that decision together.

## WHAT YOU WON'T LEARN HERE

This book is not a resource providing any "gotchas." It's a guide for best practices.

*If you're looking for loopholes, you've come to the wrong place. If you want to get a prenup and protect your connection with your partner, read on.*

If you decide a prenup is right for you, all the information you need to prepare for your prenup is within these chapters. After reading, you will be primed for a positive (and less expensive) prenup drafting experience. I've heard many well-meaning attorneys suggest couples get a prenup, trying to assure them, "You can file it away and never look at it again." In fact, that is what my attorney said to me!

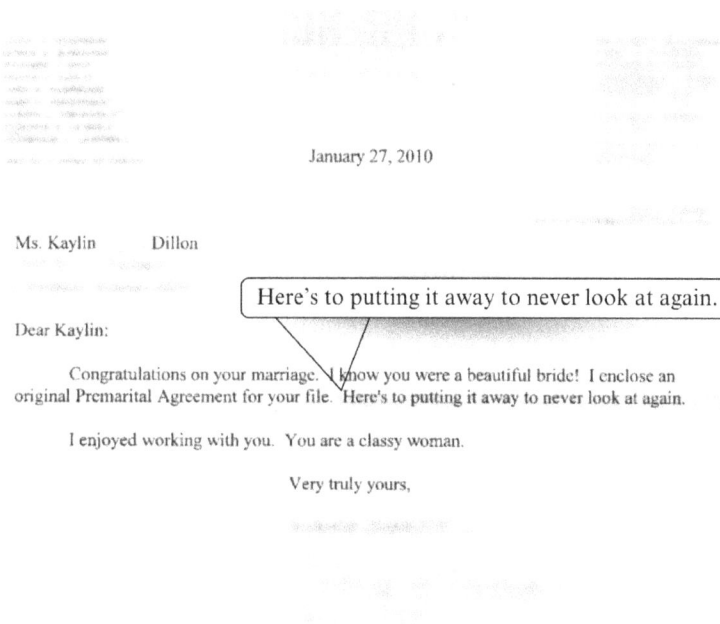

January 27, 2010

Ms. Kaylin        Dillon

Here's to putting it away to never look at again.

Dear Kaylin:

Congratulations on your marriage. I know you were a beautiful bride! I enclose an original Premarital Agreement for your file. Here's to putting it away to never look at again.

I enjoyed working with you. You are a classy woman.

Very truly yours,

Back then, I was perfectly satisfied with this suggestion, but I have a loftier goal for you. My wish is that you feel so good about your prenuptial agreement that you are happy to review it down the road.

If you meet that goal, you will set yourself up for a marriage based on healthy communication. Besides, life happens, and circumstances change. As is the case with any will or trust, it might make sense to amend a prenuptial agreement in the future. If it does, I want you to be as comfortable doing that as you are tending to any other important business in life.

# IF YOU READ NOTHING ELSE . . .

If you read nothing else, read the following—Steps for a Great Prenup. This captures the bulk of what you need to know to do this thing right.

# STEPS FOR A GREAT PRENUP

1. Make a Plan for Your Money

   - How will you split your expenses?
   - Who will fund large surprise costs?
   - How will your plan change as your income levels change?
   - How will your plan change if one of you can't (or chooses not to) work?
   - More immediately, will you each pay your own attorney's fees?

   > **Note:** The drafting attorney fee will likely cost more than the reviewing attorney fee. Ask for estimates.

2. Learn Together

   - Learn about prenups and your state laws together.
   - Your attorney may have preferred resources for you.
   - Find more helpful resources at www.kaylindillon.com.
   - Set the tone now to make this process a joint project.

3. Discuss Your Goals

   - Discuss your primary goals for your prenup together.
   - It's okay to have different goals from each other.

- Write them down, and share them with your attorney.
- Examples:
  - Simplify any potential divorce.
  - Protect a business interest.
  - Blended family considerations.
  - Protection from separate debt.
  - Keeping a family home.

4. Prepare Disclosures

- Separately, list each of your bank accounts, investment accounts, retirement accounts, properties, and anything else you own of meaningful value.
- List each of your outstanding debts.
- List anything you own or owe jointly.
- Save the related statements.

5. Draft and Review

- One attorney will draft your prenup. The other attorney will be the reviewing attorney.
- Reminder: It is your attorney's job to advocate for your individual interests. This is a good thing.
- It's up to you and your partner to communicate openly and agree wholeheartedly on your final terms.

6. Be Responsible Prenup-Havers

- Keep separate property separate. Don't mix funds from separate accounts with marital funds.

- Pay for the cost of maintaining separate property from separate funds.
- Review your prenup terms periodically. Do they still fit? Do they still feel fair?

I've spoken enough about what is to come in these next chapters. Now, I'm inviting you to join me as we go deeper into how best to have the conversations you need to procure a prenuptial agreement you and your partner can feel good about. Or you may learn through careful and compassionate exploring that a prenuptial agreement is not right for you. That's okay, too. The goal is to find out your next step and define it so the two of you can live with it.

Let's get started!

# CHAPTER 1

# Why Is Talking about Money so Hard?

---

*"While we often think of money as the domain of cold facts and rational decisions, the reality is that money is profoundly personal."*
—Amanda Clayman

THE ABILITY TO TALK ABOUT MONEY and work through uncomfortable conversations is the mark of a strong partnership.

Most people reading that statement may agree with it, but that doesn't mean any one of us is good at it—until we are instructed on how to plunge through those muddy waters and come out intact on the other side. The majority of people do not grow up hearing adults modeling healthy financial conversations, which means many people could use some practice developing this important skill.

Money is deeply personal for everyone. Broaching a conversation about how to manage finances as a couple means tapping into each other's childhoods, histories, personal values, fears, and dreams.

It's no wonder that, according to a 2019 study from the Financial Therapy Association, nearly 80% of people surveyed hadn't talked to friends or family members about money in over a year.[2]

# NAVIGATING A LOADED TOPIC

So, how do you successfully communicate about this loaded topic? The answer is: with care. It can help to have a framework that fosters the psychological safety, respect, and kindness you strive for in other aspects of your relationship. Ultimately, when you know your partner understands where you're coming from and that you care about their feelings around money, you can discuss finances constructively and with confidence—even when you don't totally agree.

Relationships fall apart when people can't talk about money. However, they don't typically disintegrate when partners disagree, so hang in there as you both work to set rules that work for each of you. Remember, disagreeing is not the death knell of your relationship; it is an invitation to tenderly explore a prickly topic and find a resolution that works for both of you.

Now, if we just had a tool to facilitate that. Wouldn't that be great?

Well, there is!

A prenup can be used to make discussing money easier. Even if you don't establish a prenup, the process of considering one lays the foundation for an ongoing discussion. And you need to be prepared. Read on to learn everything you need to know to have this poten-

---

2  Author, Guest. "14 Financial Habits That Make You Smarter with Your Money." My Financial Coach, May 3, 2022. https://myfinancialcoach.com/talking-money-with-your-partner/.

tially awkward but ultimately rewarding conversation with your partner in this chapter.

# FIRST, WHY ARE PRENUPS TRICKY?

Simply put, talking about money makes us feel vulnerable.

We are wired for connection, which is why I advise you to uncover whether or not a prenup is right for you and your partner by urging you to first talk about what you both need and want. When you go deep and lay bare what makes you the most comfortable, you reinforce your connection and foundation. You hear each other and respect each other's wishes. This is the only way to embark on this complex journey.

We may think of humans as self-interested, but science shows us that's not true. Various studies prove that neurologically, we experience our loved ones' pain in our brains, similar to how we experience direct pain ourselves.[3,4] We also know our nervous systems can regulate better if we experience pain in connection with others, which allows us to emerge from our painful experiences with fewer health and psychological consequences.

*What does sharing our pain and experiences have to do with money and prenups? Everything.*

---

3   Ucl. "Feeling Empathy for a Loved-One: Empathy for Pain Activates Pain-Sensitive Regions of the Brain, Says UCL Study." UCL News, May 6, 2022. https://www.ucl.ac.uk/news/2004/feb/feeling-empathy-loved-one-empathy-pain-activates-pain-sensitive-regions-brain-says-ucl.

4   Goldstein, Pavel, Irit Weissman-Fogel, Guillaume Dumas, and Simone G Shamay-Tsoory. "Brain-to-Brain Coupling during Handholding Is Associated with Pain Reduction." Proceedings of the National Academy of Sciences of the United States of America, March 13, 2018. https://www.ncbi.nlm.nih.gov/pmc/articles/PMC5856497/.

# THAT SENSE OF SAFETY

The fulfilling human connection we all desire in our relationship requires a sense of safety, first and foremost. And money, my friends, is always tied to our sense of safety.

In the fall of 2023, I attended a talk by Sarah Newcomb, a behavioral economist, about her latest research into what factors best predict a person's overall financial well-being.[5] Here are some of her findings:

Newcomb discovered the two most important factors for predicting a person's net worth are:

1. Age
2. Income

Not exactly groundbreaking.

However, when we look at overall financial well-being, which involves questions about how often a person feels stressed about money, whether they pay bills on time, have adequate insurance coverage, etc., the findings give us some insight to work with.

The two most important factors in predicting a person's overall financial well-being (across all levels of income and wealth) are . . .

1. Their mental time horizon (as defined by Newcomb and meaning how far ahead people think when it comes to their money)
2. How confident they feel about their finances

---

5    Newcomb, Sarah. "The Difference between Wealth and Well-Being." Morningstar, Inc., August 30, 2022. https://www.morningstar.com/financial-advisors/difference-between-wealth-well-being.

These two factors are significantly more important than income level, age, education, or gender.

Newcomb's research repeated some findings about income levels we've seen, but Newcomb spelled out some distinctions. She found that the impact of income only correlated with financial wellness until the $50,000 annual income mark. In fact, individuals earning between $75,000-150,000 with low financial confidence had a *decrease in overall financial wellness.*

Newcomb proves we have only been studying part of the story.

*"... each of us has a personal relationship with money that is largely inherited and usually unexamined and will then affect the decisions that we make with our money whether we are conscious of that or not." ~Sarah Newcomb, Ph.D., behavioral economist for Morningstar.*

Income matters when building financial wellness, but *the beliefs we hold about money and our ability to manage it are more influential.* There's also good reason to believe these concepts work in a feedback loop. Borrowing from cognitive behavioral therapy, we can deduce that you can likely improve your financial wellness by simply exercising your brain to plan on longer time horizons and build confidence around money.

We even use clues in our language around money, e.g., "safety net" and "financial security," when we reference our most fundamental needs.

Maslow's Hierarchy of Needs proves that money is required to fund the physiological needs at the bottom of the pyramid (food, shelter, and clothing) as well as the safety and security needs above that (health, secure property, safe transportation). These two tiers form the basis for our sense of well-being.[6]

The complication is that many ways of talking about money are taboo at best and, at worst, shameful in most social situations. In this way money intersects with and can threaten our sense of love and belonging, the third tier of Maslow's Hierarchy of Needs. (Money also intersects with the final two tiers of the pyramid, but let's stop here.) The point is that money can be contradictory. It is certainly complex.

# MAKE THE TIME TO TALK

These complexities and everything we've discussed make us all defensive, insecure, vulnerable, and fearful, among other emotions. This is why you must make time to have this hard conversation with your partner about money and how your futures will play out with it—together and separately.

If you're getting married, you and your fiancé or fiancée are ready to grow your sense of love and belonging by becoming a legally recognized couple. Talking about money will require you both to navigate topics and make decisions about the very elements that make up the foundation of your human needs. So, it's not uncommon for a money conversation to trigger a stress response. But this is no reason to avoid this conversation, which many couples do to preserve the peace. Think of it this way: You might stave off some uncomfortable moments but at the cost of potentially unbearable years. Trust me when I say that you can develop your skills well enough to have productive money conversations.

---

6 By, Saul Mcleod, Updated on, and January 24. "Maslow's Hierarchy of Needs." Simply Psychology, January 24, 2024. https://www.simplypsychology.org/maslow.html.

When or if the day comes that you need to refer to your prenup, it will explain each of your expectations and responsibilities. There's no arguing about it. You've already laid out the plans, and hopefully, you've been honest and have reached a satisfactory agreement on both your parts. It will save you so much time and heartache when done right.

CHAPTER 2

# Talking Money Is a Skill

---

*"Deep curiosity is a life-changing gift, something you can offer to your family, friends, colleagues, neighbors, and strangers. It's a generous force, which means it's supposed to be shared."*
—Scott Shigeoka, Seek

EMOTION REGULATION MATTERS and is a critical piece of the prenuptial puzzle because it forms the foundation for having difficult conversations. Discussing a prenuptial agreement can certainly fall into that category. Think about it; prenups often revolve around money—a topic that can trigger intense emotions. Money, much like sex or death, is one of those subjects that many of us find uncomfortable to discuss openly. It's not the kind of thing you chat about at parties, and it wasn't typically part of the conversations you had at the family dinner table while growing up.

In these conversations, our emotional gauges are often misaligned. We're not sure what's normal or abnormal, and we tend to put our defenses up quickly. Misinterpretations abound. When it comes to prenuptial agreements, someone might become more sensitive or feel threatened because money is a vital resource that affects our sense of security.

# THE WINDOW OF TOLERANCE

Now, let me introduce you to a concept that can be truly transformative: the "window of tolerance." This idea changed how my husband and I communicate, whether we're talking about money or anything else.

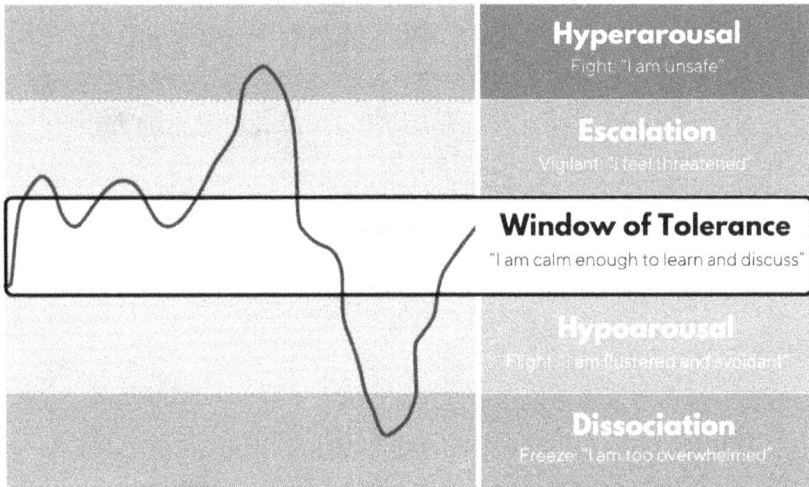

Your window of tolerance is the range of emotions you can comfortably handle. It's the emotional space where you can think clearly, make rational decisions, and respond thoughtfully rather than impulsively. When you step outside this window, whether your emotions skyrocket or plummet, your brain loses full access to the frontal lobe, where all good decision-making happens.

You might hear this state referred to as fight or flight or as being dysregulated. Whatever you call it, what's important to understand for financial conversations is that in this state where your brain is hyper-focused on survival and safety, complex thinking and rational discussions are nearly impossible. You tend to see things in black and white so that everything can feel like a life-or-death situation.

Have you ever remembered a recent, tense conversation completely differently than your partner? Odds are good one or both of you was operating outside your window of tolerance.

# RECOGNIZING THE SIGNS

Before you engage in a conversation about a prenuptial agreement, keep an eye out for signs that someone is outside of their window of tolerance. These signs might include heightened emotions, such as anger or sadness, defensiveness, irrationality, or withdrawal.

It's crucial to understand that when you spot these signs, it doesn't matter how well you presented your case or how gently you broached the subject. Nothing will be productive in that moment. It's a clear signal to pause, step back, and try your conversation again at a more opportune time.

Now, I know advising that you not talk about money when someone is worked up or shutting down sounds simple, but following this advice can be challenging, especially if you're not accustomed to recognizing and managing emotions in this way. Yet, developing this skill is vital. You need your prefrontal cortex, the part of your brain responsible for wise decision-making, to be active during these conversations. When you're in fight or flight mode, you're operating from what some call the "lizard brain," which is a part of your brain that concentrates on basic survival instincts.

While it might seem a bit unconventional to start a discussion about prenuptial agreements while striving for emotion regulation and getting your lizard brain to chill, it's a fundamental step that cannot be skipped. Understanding and practicing emotion regulation will not only make your discussions about prenups more productive, but it can also enhance communication in every aspect of your relationship. One approach works best over any other: Be curious and open.

Like any new skill, learning to be curious and open works best when you practice mastering the basics first. One of the key basics in talking about money is to approach the topic first with curiosity and a desire to learn more about your partner's feelings around various money topics.

Here's a tip that might seem counterintuitive: Keep the conversation in healthy curiosity mode by agreeing upfront to take decision-making off the table. Most often, we only talk about money when a decision needs to be made, but there is plenty to talk about beyond those business-of-life decisions we're usually focused on. Not sure what that even looks like? I'll share some prompts after these tips.

Before either of you speak one word, it's important to look for signals that somebody is outside their window of tolerance. When people get outside this window, they make impulsive decisions. If you see the conversation is about to take a turn that will be hard to recover from, remember it doesn't matter who's right or wrong. It doesn't matter if you presented the facts and what you need really well or if you were so gentle in bringing up this topic. Again, pause, back off, and try again at a better time.

If you're not used to assessing and regulating your emotions and helping your partner do the same based on signals you're also learning to see, it can be very difficult to do in practice. That's okay. Don't give up.

As Julia Rodgers, founder of HelloPrenup, notes: "When you're having the prenup conversation, what you're having a conversation about is your life trajectory together. What's that going to look like?"

# BEFORE TALKING MONEY, CONSIDER THESE TIPS:

- Set aside time to talk in advance.
- Make sure you're both comfortable and at ease. (No hangry money talks!)
- Keep it short enough that you'll want to do it again.
- Make it your goal to be purely curious about your partner's responses and feelings.
- Take decision-making off the table. Thorough discussions are best treated as exploratory missions, not business meetings.
- Call it off if it gets too tense, and circle back with refreshed gentleness and curiosity when it feels like a better time.

Here are a few questions to get your wheels turning:

1. What's your earliest money memory?
   *Early memories help us identify our most deeply ingrained impressions about the role of money in our lives.*

2. What's important about money to you?
   *This question helps you start to think about what you want to prioritize in your financial life.*

3. How was money saved, managed, and allocated in your family growing up? How did your family view and talk about money?
   *This talking point is a tool to help you clarify existing beliefs and habits—necessary to start moving forward and have more in-depth, constructive conversations.*

23

4. Are there financial topics or expenses you consider private? Why do you feel this way?
   *Answer this question to help you notice preferences and unspoken expectations you each have about certain financial topics.*

5. What scares you about combining finances?
   *Learn what you both might need to feel secure.*

6. Have you ever felt like you had enough money? When and why was this?
   *This question helps you start to notice under what conditions you feel secure with money.*

7. What's the biggest financial decision you've made? How did you make that decision? Who did you turn to for advice?
   *Reviewing big financial decisions of the past can help us sort out what parts of our past decision-making process we want to keep and what parts we might want to change as we form new decision-making customs together.*

8. If money were no object, what would your ideal life look like? What does financial success mean to you if you can achieve it? How would you know you've arrived at it?
   *Exploring this question gives your mind more possibilities and can help get to the root of your financial desires and goals.*

9. What's one thing you would change about the way we manage our money?
   *Knowing the answer to this question sets a baseline and gives you both a chance to share concerns and wishes, so you can start aligning on a shared future vision.*

10. What would you like money to do for us that we haven't done yet?

*Discussing this may help you develop more tangible action items that can help you on your way to your shared vision.*

If you really dove in, you might have only made it through one question on this list. That's great! If your first go at an in-depth money discussion didn't feel like a great success, that's all right, too. Go easy on yourselves. This is new territory, and you have a lifetime ahead to keep trying.

Understand, those 10 questions were just a start. You were simply feeling out each other's emotions to see where you stand.

Having conversations about money is challenging. Having a healthy mindset around money is essential for your relationship. Hidden fears and concerns can slowly take their toll, and conversations can shine a light on them, enabling you to resolve them together. Communication is vital in all relationships, and it should extend into the financial side of your relationship.

# EMOTION REGULATION

## HYPERAROUSAL
### Fight or Flight

Looks like:
- racing heart
- frazzled or frantic thoughts
- urge to run or fight
- sweating
- fast breathing
- difficulty sleeping

## WINDOW OF TOLERANCE

*The emotional comfort zone.
The ideal state for
communicating, learning,
and decision-making.*

Looks like:
- calm
- alert
- focused
- engaged
- curious
- relaxed

## HYPOAROUSAL
### Fawn, Freeze, Flop

Looks like:
- disengagement
- low energy
- dissociation from emotions
- low level of responsiveness
- lower heart rate
- slower breathing

# CHAPTER 3

# Money Conversations to Have Before Marriage

---

*"Without leaps of imagination or dreaming, we lose the excitement of possibilities. Dreaming, after all, is a form of planning."*
—Gloria Steinem

NOW THAT YOU'VE GOT A SENSE of how the two of you will do in your discussion and the window of tolerance to watch for let's make sure you're covering the essential money conversations to have before saying, "I do." Beyond your past experiences with money, these marriage prep topics will give you insight into each other's financial philosophies, hopes, and ambitions.

These pre-wedding convos should help you start to form a joint vision for your finances. Make time to commit to discovering some key facts about how you both view money and other associated financial necessities.

# BIG PICTURE

- What are your individual career and personal goals?
- What are the financial goals you want to reach together? Do you hope to quit your nine-to-fives by age 50 or have a vacation home in Boca?
- What do you want the experience of pursuing your goals to be like? Intense? Pleasurable? Something else?
- How do you feel about your finances currently?
- What do you anticipate are likely areas of financial stress for you?
- What does having "enough" money look like to each of you?
- What are your views on charitable giving? Would you like to make this a priority?

I recommend prioritizing your own financial health first. A financial plan can help you determine how much you can afford to give away while staying well enough on track to meet your financial goals. More on that later.

- What's your philosophy on debt?

It's important to talk about your plans to pay off debt, as this is an area where people tend to have strong emotions. If you grew up hearing about the importance of being debt-free or saw your family experience difficulties due to family debt, you might care deeply about getting rid of your debt as soon as it comes in. Conversely, if you don't feel panicky or uneasy carrying debt, you might want to pay off your loans over time—even if your partner offers to pay them for you.

Regardless of your situation, foster an open dialogue about debt to feel confident that the long-term plans you make together are realistic and take both of your concerns into account.

# HYPOTHETICALS

- How would you manage if one of you fell ill and couldn't work?
- How will you address conflicts around your individual goals? Will one person's career take precedence?
- What are your hopes or expectations around relying on financial support from family or being able to provide financial support to family in times of need?

# PURCHASES

- What purchases are important to you (like travel or hobbies)?
- What do you think is a huge waste of money (like Uber Eats or buying new cars)?
- Are you planning on making any major expenditures in the near future (such as buying a home, making home improvements, or investing in education)? Develop your plan now to ensure adequate funding.
- How do you feel about credit cards? What have your credit card habits been like in the past?
- What do you consider a "large" purchase? Is there a set amount you can both spend without asking the other person first?

Lots of couples set a maximum guilt-free purchase amount so they don't have to discuss every single purchase they make.

Don't feel like you need to have the same answer. Most couples don't. Again, strive to be on the same page. It's rare for couples to have identical views on money, including how best to spend it. In fact, in their 40 years of research, relationship experts Drs. John and Julie Gottman have found that *how* a couple talks about their financial disagreements matters far more than agreeing with one another.[7]

When you work on your money conversations and commit to getting the essential questions answered, over time, you can move toward more similar views. Take a healthy interest in your spouse's reasoning for their particular priorities, yet understand that it's perfectly normal to have different values and beliefs about money.

# THE "LITTLE" TOPICS MATTER

Any monthly expense you disagree about needs addressing. It will come up over and over in your relationship. While you're at it, discuss your feelings around late fees and ATM and overdraft fees. You're not trying to find a solution in your conversation at this point; it's more that you want to know the sensitive issues affecting the two of you. One person may feel strong shame tied to their experiences of incurring an overdraft fee regardless of their financial situation, for instance. Another may feel they are just busy and doing the best they can—they can tolerate it as long as they are generally in good shape financially.

---

7    Gottman, John; Gottman, Julie Schwartz; Abrams, Doug; Abrams, Rachel Carlton. *Eight dates essential conversations for a lifetime of Love.* S.l.: Workman Publishing Company, 2019.

# FAMILY

- *Do you plan on having children and want either one of you to stay home to raise them?* When you answer this question, keep in mind how it will affect your ability to pay for a major purchase (such as a house) and maintain your lifestyle on one income.

- Do you plan to pay for your kids' college? If so, would you want to foot the bill for all/some/none of it?

> **Note:** Paying for college is the number one topic couples openly disagree about in my office.

# REGARDING COMPROMISES

Get each other's takes on these important topics early on when the stakes are low. Then, before making any compromises on items of misalignment, pause and check first for understanding.

Let's take the college expenses example. If one spouse wants to pay for college and one does not, you may want to consider splitting the cost, but there is an inherent problem with this option.

If one spouse thinks they should pay for their child's college because she believes that's what set her up for success in life, and the other thinks paying his own way through college is what led to his great work ethic, deciding on a compromise, like paying for 50% of your kids' college, is going to leave both spouses feeling like they're under-preparing their children for life.

Instead of feeling like a compromise, it might feel a lot more like a total loss for each of them. This is why what's critical at this hypothetical stage is to learn about where each of you is coming from. That way, any compromises or solutions you come up with down the road can actually address your underlying concerns. For example, maybe this example couple would feel better about paying for the first year of college only or setting grade requirements for their children before covering tuition.

No matter the topic, if you start to strongly disagree, revisit your talk at later dates. Address your partner with kindness and genuine curiosity to find out their reasoning behind why they value what they do so highly. You might think their opinions are shallow or silly, but if you dig a little deeper, you'll probably learn that real logic is attached to their feelings and is actually quite understandable, even if you disagree.

*If you can learn more about your partner's "why," your money discussions might even deepen your connection and trust.*

Talking about money is hard, but avoiding it is harder in the end, and it is just as vital to your relationship as any other type of communication. It also takes practice. Start small, and build confidence and trust before moving on to bigger conversations. If you're both willing to practice the skill of discussing money, you're already off to a fantastic start.

Let me leave you with a final thought on this topic: *Why not discuss what you two think is fair at a time when your relationship is at a peak affection level?*

# SET COLLABORATIVE GOALS

If you're new to setting collaborative financial goals, start with one you can control. For example, a great first couple's goal could be to review your monthly spending together.

If you've created trust and comfort, it may be possible to manage difficult goals together. These could be prioritizing paying down debt or building up an emergency savings fund. If your individual finances are in good shape, you can better define your life goals, such as saving for your kids' college education, buying your dream home, or figuring out a retirement plan.

When you set goals together, you get buy-in from both sides. Each person is allowed to express their thoughts and opinions, ultimately allowing you to find common ground and work toward your goals in a unified manner.

It's important not to neglect individual financial goals as you work to make plans for the two of you. You may have a joint checking account for standard household spending but separate accounts for your spending, for instance. Having conversations around what you each value creates transparency, easing potential concerns around what your collective and individual money is being used for. It works even better when you practice emotion regulation.

After setting goals, you need a plan to reach them. Once you've had conversations and highlighted some key goals, get out a pen and paper (or a Google Doc) and write them down. Don't let your progress go to waste by not following through on previously discussed goals and action items. While the plan isn't going to be perfect, and adjustments will need to be made over time, these steps serve as a starting point to move in the right direction.

Unsure how to actually plan for those goals? Hang tight. I have steps for creating your first joint financial plan coming up.

# CHAPTER 4

# Merging Finances

---

*"The single biggest problem in communication is
the illusion it has taken place."*
—George Bernard Shaw

AS YOU PLAN TO MERGE YOUR LIVES, consider how you'll
handle your finances together. Where will you be depositing income
going forward? In essence, where will the money go?

There's no right or wrong regarding how you merge your money,
per se, so long as you:

1. Create a setup that fits with your prenup if you get one. (More
   on how to do this coming later.)
2. Communicate about your approach intentionally, so it feels
   right to both of you.

You can choose to maintain separate accounts, open joint accounts, or find a combination that works for you.

By the way, have you decided how you'll split expenses?

For better or for worse, your marriage is a financial partnership.

Still, many engaged couples aren't sure how they want to combine their finances during marriage.

What are the options and best practices?

What's a fair way to split expenses?

Should we get a prenup?

The questions quickly become overwhelming. People often shake them off and avoid them altogether.

*They might waive off their own concerns, saying, "None of those money questions have anything to do with love and marriage. Right?"*

By now, you know my feeling on this subject: Following those questions through to arrive at the answers you need will serve your marriage well.

More than that, there are beautiful tokens of connection and trust buried under those money questions, just waiting for you two to reach them together.

# OPTIONS FOR SPLITTING EXPENSES

Here are some different ways couples split expenses if you need a few ideas.

### 1. 50/50

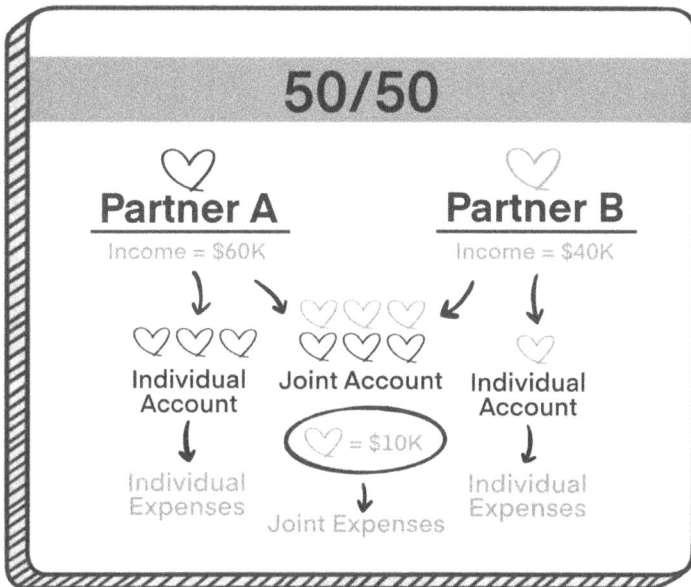

50/50

Partner A
Income = $60K

Partner B
Income = $40K

Individual Account

Joint Account

Individual Account

= $10K

Individual Expenses

Joint Expenses

Individual Expenses

Each partner deposits a fixed, equal amount into a joint account monthly. Then, you will both pay agreed-upon expenses from the joint account. All other income is deposited into individual accounts.

This option is pretty easy to set up and understand. It works best for couples who earn roughly the same amount of money.

## 2. Proportional to Income

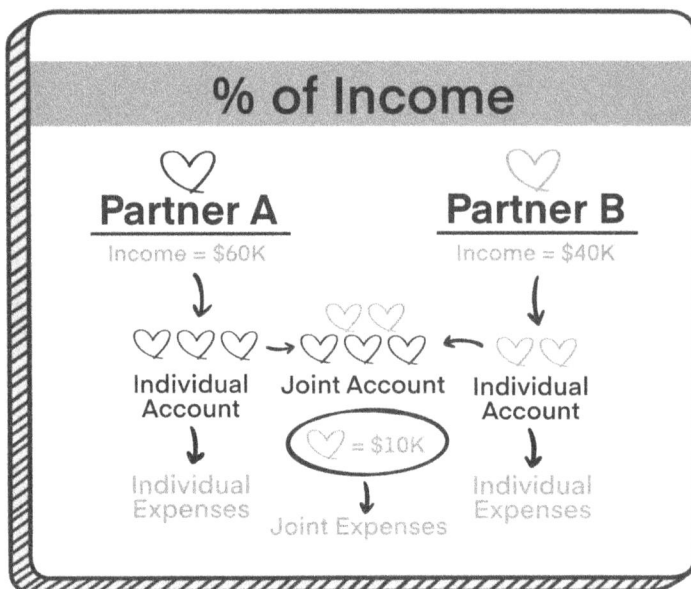

With this plan, you will split joint expenses based on each partner's share of the total combined income: e.g., Partner A, making a $120k salary, pays 60%, and Partner B, making $80k, pays 40%. Individual expenses can still be paid from individual accounts.

This option tends to be a good fit for dual-income newlyweds, particularly if you have a significant difference in income. This way, the spouse earning less money isn't disproportionately burdened by the shared expenses.

> **Note:** Remember that income is not just your salary. It can also include investment income, trust distributions, cash gifts, etc.

## 3. Category Based

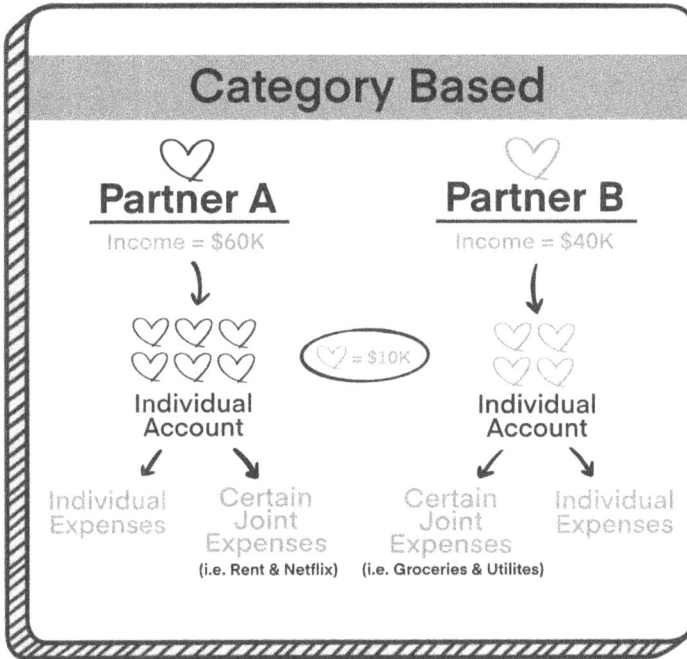

Define whether an expense is an individual or joint expense based on category, e.g., one partner owns the home and pays the mortgage and home maintenance from individual funds while the other partner pays for groceries and restaurant tabs.

> **Note:** Don't use this system. This tends to be the accidental setup that couples fall into because they didn't make an intentional plan for *splitting expenses*. This regimen ends up being the murkiest and hardest to revise over time as costs *and* income levels change.

## 4. Allowance Based

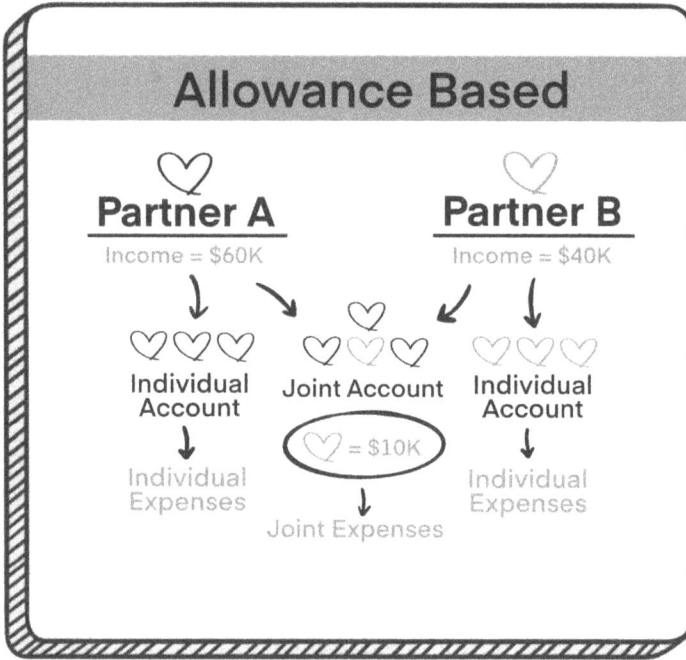

**Allowance Based**

Partner A
Income = $60K

Partner B
Income = $40K

Individual Account

Joint Account

Individual Account

= $10K

Individual Expenses

Joint Expenses

Individual Expenses

Deposit a fixed dollar amount into each individual account monthly. This works like an "allowance" for each partner to use freely or save up. Other income is deposited into a joint account. In effect, joint expenses are split based on each partner's percentage of the total income.

What makes the allowance approach different is that it guarantees the amount each partner gets in their individual account monthly is equal, regardless of who makes more money.

This is a great option for couples with kids. As soon as you have a child, there's plenty of unpaid labor to go around! It makes sense to allocate the same amount of money to each partner for their independent use.

## 5. 100% Joint

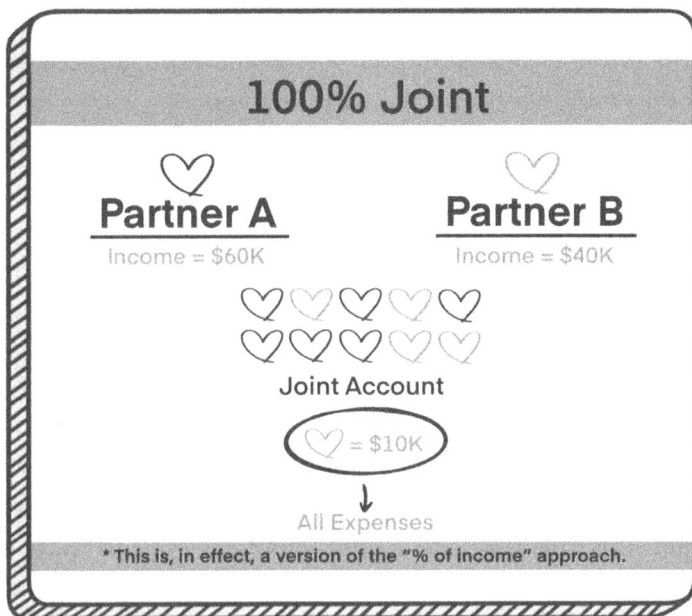

Combine all income into a joint account and fund all expenses from that account. No individual accounts. You can each use separate credit cards for gifts or private purchases if agreed. In effect, all expenses are split based on each partner's percentages of the total income.

There are lots of ways to slice the cookie. What matters is that your method for managing expenses is decided upon together and that you will both continue to use it as long as you feel it is working well for you. If you're not sure where to begin, agree to revisit any decisions at set times to assess what is and isn't working. (This advice applies to all topic areas!)

> **Note:** Even if you decide to keep individual accounts, the money you make during your marriage and deposit in those accounts will likely be considered marital property unless you have a prenuptial agreement stating otherwise. Learn more about this in a later chapter.

# INSURANCE

Getting married will impact your insurance needs and options. Here are a few of the items you'll want to consider.

Are you both on employer-sponsored health plans?

If so, one health plan may be more advantageous than the other, or it might even make sense to stay on separate plans, believe it or not. Find this out, and take action before you have to wait another year or will be ineligible to make any changes to the policy, as there is a limited window to enroll after a qualifying event. The Qualifying Life Event (QLE) window to change your health insurance after you get married is at least 30 days for employer health plans, and you have 60 days after your marriage to enroll in the Health Insurance Marketplace.[8]

Tips for comparing health plans:

1. Compare the plans, assuming you both have a year of high health expenses and a year of low health expenses. Your scenario comparisons should include an instance where you each stay on your own company plans and an instance where you enroll as a family on each of your company plans.

---

8   "Getting Health Coverage Outside Open Enrollment." HealthCare.gov. Accessed July 14, 2024. https://www.healthcare.gov/coverage-outside-open-enrollment/special-enrollment-period/.

2. Look at your premium cost in addition to your anticipated expenses under each plan. And *add* back into the calculation any free money you get in the form of employer contributions to a Health Savings Account, Health Reimbursement Account, or Flexible Spending Account.

3. Include the relevant tax savings from any deductible Health Savings Account contributions—and don't forget you likely have a new annual contribution limit if you're enrolling as a family instead of as an individual.

4. Keep in mind that it's not a given that you should be on the same health plan. Sometimes, the premium for one individual is so much lower than it is for a couple that it makes sense to stay on separate plans. On the other hand, sometimes the family deductible is a better deal, meaning it makes sense to be on the same plan even though your employers cover almost all of your individual premiums. Hence, it's really worth digging into the scenario comparisons.

# TAX PLANNING

Tax planning is an important component of merging your financial lives. Generally speaking, it's more advantageous for most couples to file joint taxes than it is to file separate taxes. But this is not a reliable rule of thumb. Confirm the best filing strategy for you with your accountant. Be sure to ask your accountant to confirm which tax deductions or benefits change as a result of filing jointly, and communicate to your accountant details of any income-based student loan repayment program or other income-based benefits you count on.

> **Note:** You can file a joint tax return for a given tax year so long as you were married by Dec. 31st of that year.[9]

Additionally, you want to confirm you're making contributions to the right type of tax-advantaged account (aka "retirement account") for your new tax status. For example, if you've been making Roth IRA contributions in the past, you'll need to make sure you still qualify to make direct Roth contributions based on your combined income. Alternatively, if your income was too high to make direct Roth contributions previously, filing joint taxes could put you back under the income limit, allowing you to make those contributions.

> **Note:** If either of you make estimated tax payments quarterly, update your payment amounts according to your new joint estimates. Yes, you need to do this before your first joint return is filed.[10]

# CREDIT

Let's talk about what happens to your credit when you get married. You might be surprised to know that your credit isn't automatically affected by your spouse's credit.

9    "Tax To-Dos for Newlyweds to Keep in Mind." n.d. Irs.gov. Accessed July 27, 2024. https://www.irs.gov/newsroom/tax-to-dos-for-newlyweds-to-keep-in-mind.

10    See relevant tax filing instructions in form 2210. Source: "Instructions for Form 2210." 2023. Irs.gov. 2023. https://www.irs.gov/pub/irs-pdf/i2210.pdf.

Here are some things that do affect your credit:

- A joint loan, like a mortgage, will impact both of your credit scores for better or for worse.
- A credit card will impact the primary holder's credit for better or for worse BUT only helps the credit of the additional cardholder (i.e., spouse), and it helps to a lesser extent than it does for the primary cardholder.[11]

This next part is really important ….

*If you are not the primary cardholder, you're not building up as much good credit as your spouse is.*

You can both use the same card for years and make all the payments on time, and only that primary holder gets full credit for the good behavior (pun intended). It also means you shouldn't get dinged if the primary holder misses a payment.

Make sure BOTH of you have a credit card as the primary cardholder so you're both getting credit for all your good payments! And if a spouse is spending more on their card than you can afford, make sure they're doing it as a primary cardholder, not as an additional cardholder on your account.

> **Note:** Nothing in a prenup or divorce agreement can directly impact your credit report. Your prenup can say the new debt you take out is separate, but you totally negate that if you take it out in joint name.

---

11    Friedman, Pam. *I now pronounce you financially fit: How to protect your money in marriage and divorce.* Austin: River Grove Books, 2015.

# THOUGHTS ON MERGING FINANCES

It doesn't matter how you set up your accounts or how you split expenses. Having separate money shouldn't impede you two from marching toward your goals as a team. What matters is that you set your finances up with intention together.

However you architect your joint finances, make sure you have the correct expenses coming out of the right accounts. If you agree to split utilities, pay the utilities out of a joint account. Couples run into the most confusing scenarios when they too frequently reimburse each other.

That said, one of my couples does successfully track their expenses in a spreadsheet monthly and then reimburses each other via Venmo. It can work, but this couple is certainly the exception.

You know your relationship best. Are you both equally excited about spreadsheets? Great. If not—or you'd rather do something else with your time, set yourself up for success and less work by using the following checklist to agree on which expenses are paid out of which account type.

> **Note:** Email the final version of this list to your partner and confirm they agree with it. This way, you can reference it later if you forget. Plan to review it at least annually to make sure it still feels right and fair to both of you.*

# COUPLE'S EXPENSE PLANNER

Joint expenses should be paid from a joint account. Individual expenses should be paid from individual accounts. Use this planner to plan which of your expenses will be considered joint expenses and which ones you'll consider individual expenses. Then, make sure your payment settings are set up to draft from the right account type.

| Category | Partner 1 Account | Joint Account | Partner 2 Account | Updated auto payment info? ✓ |
|---|---|---|---|---|
| Mortgage/Rent | ☐ | ☐ | ☐ | ☐ |
| Car Payment | ☐ | ☐ | ☐ | ☐ |
| Insurance | ☐ | ☐ | ☐ | ☐ |
| Utilities | ☐ | ☐ | ☐ | ☐ |
| Recurring Medical | ☐ | ☐ | ☐ | ☐ |
| Automatic Savings | ☐ | ☐ | ☐ | ☐ |
| Childcare | ☐ | ☐ | ☐ | ☐ |
| Home Maintenance | ☐ | ☐ | ☐ | ☐ |
| Subscriptions | ☐ | ☐ | ☐ | ☐ |
| Memberships | ☐ | ☐ | ☐ | ☐ |
| Recurring Personal | ☐ | ☐ | ☐ | ☐ |
| Groceries | ☐ | ☐ | ☐ | |
| Gas | ☐ | ☐ | ☐ | |
| Personal | ☐ | ☐ | ☐ | |
| Entertainment | ☐ | ☐ | ☐ | |
| Restaurants | ☐ | ☐ | ☐ | |
| Gifts | ☐ | ☐ | ☐ | |
| Cash Spending | ☐ | ☐ | ☐ | |
| Travel | ☐ | ☐ | ☐ | |
| Car Repairs | ☐ | ☐ | ☐ | |
| Home Repair | ☐ | ☐ | ☐ | |
| Holiday Spending | ☐ | ☐ | ☐ | |
| Auto Insurance | ☐ | ☐ | ☐ | ☐ |
| Annual Subscriptions | ☐ | ☐ | ☐ | ☐ |
| Other | ☐ | ☐ | ☐ | |

# CHAPTER 5

# Your Premarital Financial Plan

*"Plans are nothing; planning is everything."*
—Dwight D. Eisenhower

THE KEY to getting your premarital money decisions "right" is to build your joint vision for your future together. There's no better way to do that than by writing your first joint financial plan. Doing so helps you as a couple to feel supported and encourages you to be true partners while navigating the tough conversations about who should pay for what, how that will need to change if you have kids, etc.

Approaching these needed conversations means by the time we discuss the pros and cons of a prenup, my couples are ready to consider their options with care. If they decide to go forward with a prenup, I prepare and guide them through the process to be sure this remains a joint project they can feel good about.

If you're asking these questions, you're already on the right track to a healthier relationship. The only way to do it wrong is NOT to have the tough conversations that go with them.

Take a proactive approach, and you can lay a solid foundation for a prosperous life as a married couple.

# START WITH THE BASICS

## To Budget or Not to Budget

Developing a budgeting strategy may not sound exciting, but it's an essential step in managing your finances as a couple. The good news is that it does not always have to be labor intensive, and you may already be in a financial situation where you can skip straight to not budgeting, aka "reverse budgeting."

The right approach for your financial plan depends on your situation (and your personality!). Usually, when I start working with clients, they first want to know if I will make them track a monthly itemized budget. Tracking an itemized budget monthly is what I call "traditional budgeting." The odds are good that, unless you were already following a monthly itemized budget before you became a client, one of the more hands-off approaches I am about to share with you will be a better fit for your plan.

1. Traditional Budgeting
2. Reverse Budgeting
3. Flow-Based Budgeting

Here's a little about each of these types of budgets so you can determine the best one to work for you.

# TRADITIONAL BUDGETING

**Optimal for** those who need to stretch a low or fixed income every month.

**Overview**: When people hear "budgeting," they usually think of Traditional Budgeting, which requires individuals to outline their expected income and expenses for the month and set intended limits for each category of expenses. This sort of detailed budgeting works best with a tracking app.

## Pros:

- Provides a detailed understanding of spending habits.
- Helps identify areas of highest spending.
- Can be tailored to specific financial goals, such as debt payoff or saving for a particular purpose.

## Cons:

- Requires consistent attention and discipline to maintain.
- Can feel restrictive.
- Can be overwhelming.

# RECOMMENDED TRACKING APPS:

- **Monarch Money**

  My husband and I used Mint for 12 years, and I loved that it was low-maintenance and free. It let us see guidelines and trends, but it also made it easy to jump back in if we fell off the wagon for a while. We started using Monarch Money when Mint announced its retirement in 2023, and we find it even more user-friendly. You can set a strict budget by category in Monarch Money, or you can use it simply to view trends. It's a good complement to any of the three budgeting approaches I'm outlining here. Monarch Money is a great tool for budgeting lovers and haters alike. I've started using it with my clients, too, and it's particularly good for couples who keep separate accounts but want to view the full picture together.

- **YNAB**

  If you're ready for a more cutthroat approach to budgeting, I recommend YNAB (You Need A Budget). This app shows no mercy! If you overspend in a category, you'll get a pop-up asking you which other category you want to reduce to account for the overspending. You can only click out of this pop-up to review your budget after you decide! On the plus side, YNAB has a strong community of budgeting experts online (primarily on Reddit). Community can go a long way in helping you through a tough budgeting transition if you need to make drastic changes.

---

**Note:** Both of these apps cost money. As much as I'd love to have a great free suggestion, I haven't found one yet. RIP Mint. If you're adamant you've found a useful and free budgeting tool, I'd love to hear about it. Contact me at www.kaylindillon.com.

---

# REVERSE BUDGETING

**Optimal for** those who are already saving enough toward their financial goals.

**Overview:** Reverse budgeting focuses on savings goals. Instead of starting with expenses, you'll figure out how much you need to save monthly to meet your retirement, college, travel, and other goals. If you're meeting those savings goals monthly, there's only a need to track where the rest of the money is going *if you want to*. Set up automatic account transfers to meet your monthly savings goals without fail, then ensure those funds also invest automatically, if appropriate.

## Pros:

- Hands off. Very little time or maintenance is required.
- Guarantees a specific saving rate.
- Provides flexibility for discretionary spending.

## Cons:

- Doesn't provide a detailed understanding of spending habits.
- Only works if you have excess cash flow every month.

# FLOW-BASED BUDGETING

**Optimal for** those wondering, "Where does the money go?" each month.

**Overview:** Flow-based budgeting is all about narrowing the scope of money decisions. I was introduced to this concept at a financial planning conference in 2023 by presenter Natalie Taylor. Instead of looking at your "needs" vs. "wants" in your budget, flow-based budgeting assesses what is automated versus what requires you to make an active decision.

## Pros:

- Simplifies decision-making: If there's money in the spending account, you can splurge; if not, you wait.
- Weekly refresh provides a clean slate, which can be encouraging for those who might have overspent in the past.
- Reduces the need for continuous tracking.

## Cons:

- May not be meticulous enough for those who need to pay down debt under a particular timeline.
- Those with irregular income may struggle to determine the right weekly amount.
- May require some extra setup time to open new accounts and change payment information.

# HOW FLOW-BASED BUDGETING WORKS

Designate three different accounts or cards for the following three categories.

1. **Fixed Account:** AKA the monthly autopay account. This account is for monthly commitments already on autopay, like your mortgage, subscriptions, and utilities. This account is also for standing commitments you've made, even if there isn't a true autopayment set up. For instance, it would work well for bi-weekly therapy appointments.

2. **Flex Account:** AKA the weekly spending account. This account is for expenses that require an intentional purchase, i.e., groceries, gas, shopping, etc. Make an initial estimate of weekly expenses, add some cushion to it, and replenish the account each Saturday. You'll likely need to adjust the amount a time or two as you get up and running.

3. **Non-Monthly Account:** This account is for expenses that tend to recur annually or sporadically and are larger and may or may not be on autopay. Examples include property taxes, holiday spending, car repairs, and annual travel.

If you want to do this with separate credit cards instead of separate accounts, pay down the flex spending card every Saturday to reset the spending amount. The main goal is that once you're set up and humming along, all you need to reference for your spending decisions is the balance in that flex spending account (or on that card). It's much easier for your brain to decide if you can afford something if all you have to do is look at the balance of one account.

## Tips:

1. If you need to cut your spending, you'll still have to trim expenses from your fixed account.
2. If you set up a new subscription in the fixed account, reduce your transfers to the weekly spending account accordingly.
3. If you and your partner have separate accounts, set up separate fixed accounts, flex accounts, etc. Or set up a different combination that mimics the setup you have now.

Budgeting is personal. What works for one person may not work for another. The key is to find an approach that aligns with your goals, lifestyle, and temperament. Whether it's the detail-oriented approach of traditional budgeting, the savings-first mindset of reverse budgeting, or the simplicity of flow-based budgeting, you can find a strategy to help you take control of your finances.

# SPREADSHEETS VERSUS ONLINE TOOLS

While a spreadsheet works just fine for many people, I find that online tools are optimal for couples and give them consistent access to the same updated information.

# SAVINGS

## Build an Emergency Fund

Building an emergency fund together helps you handle unexpected expenses or financial setbacks. Aim to save three to six months' worth of living expenses in this emergency fund. Aim even higher if either of you deals with uncertain compensation or job security concerns.

## Savings for Short-Term Goals

In addition to an emergency fund, you also want to save enough money to fund large expenditures you'll have in the next 1-2 years. For example, if you have an emergency fund with six months' worth of living expenses already saved up, but you know you plan to buy a house in the next couple of years, start saving up your down payment in addition to those funds.

These savings amounts can go into the same account or stay in separate accounts. I personally like Ally for savings. Their high-yield savings account consistently offers competitive interest rates on savings, and their account "buckets" feature lets you keep your money in one account while earmarking certain amounts for different goals. Many other online-only savings banks have similar features.

# LONG-TERM PLANNING

*Committing plans in writing is powerful.*

Now that you've covered the basics and set up a savings plan for short-term goals, you're ready to talk about your larger financial plans. In addition to making plans to achieve your big, long-term goals, your money plan can consist of many different elements, like outlining financial responsibilities for the household, who pays the bills, when you'll review spending choices together, or who manages the investments. It's not uncommon for partners to think the other is handling a task, so it's worth checking together to ensure the lines of responsibility are clear and that everyone's comfortable with their current "chores."

If you're one of the many busy couples that operate by addressing "fires" like past-due notices and tax deadlines as they come up, your schedules and stress levels will benefit greatly if you discuss responsibilities clearly and give yourselves room to divide and conquer financial tasks proactively.

## Set Your Joint Goals

Use the skills you've honed talking about money to discuss your long-term priorities. What major purchases do you hope to make? What do you want your working life and retirement life to look like?

One simple way to set a long-term savings goal is to use a free online tool to estimate how much you want to save now for retirement. When people ask me about my favorite free tools, I usually suggest the Vanguard Income Retirement Calculator. It couldn't be easier to use, and it gets the job done when it comes to figuring out how much you should deposit into your retirement accounts and what you can spend when the time comes to use it. If you don't like the output, play with the numbers until you do.

## Invest for Your Future

The most important step you can take for your long-term finances is to save and invest regularly to build your nest egg. Even if you can't afford to save the ideal amount right now, start as small as you need to. Just remember, any amount you invest for the long-term should be an amount you plan to leave invested for the next 15-20 years or more.

*The details of our real lives vary greatly from investor to investor. Be wary of following any rules of thumb based solely on your income.*

For example, if two people earn $150,000 and save 20% per year, that might be more than enough for someone who starts early, plans to work until 70, and lives in a low-cost area in the Midwest. It likely won't work for someone who wants to retire at 50 in a major city and anticipates needing to support their parents with a high risk of health issues.

## Financial Planning

Lastly, a financial planner can help you make the most of each level of financial management. We do more thorough tax planning and insurance analysis and assess how your financial plan fits with your estate plan. We can also help you assess what type of retirement account you should take advantage of based on your situation.

If you're not ready to get into the weeds with a long-term plan, I get it. Address what you can right now, and turn back to a financial plan when you're thinking about buying a house, considering a job change, or starting to plan for kids and their education.

# ARE YOU READY TO INVEST?

Before you put your first penny away, make sure your financial priorities are in order.

Average investment returns won't outrun the interest rate on a credit card. If poor spending habits put you in a hole, making a long-term investment is like signing up for a 10k before mastering the mile. You don't need full marathon-level skills to invest, but you do need to have the basic mile down. In other words, you need to make enough money and have and apply the basic skills to be sure you aren't running a monthly deficit.

You might be eager to invest, but you're more likely to lose money investing if you have no savings cushion to rely on in a pinch. This is when investing is more like gambling.

## Check Before You Invest

1. **Credit Card Debt:** Do you have credit card debt? If so, prioritize paying it down monthly.

2. **Emergency Savings:** Once you've eliminated your credit card debt, divert that monthly payment to a savings account until you have at least 3-6 months of living expenses saved.

3. **Regular Savings:** After you have emergency savings accrued, build up additional funds for any major purchases or expenses you know are coming in the next 1-2 years. The bigger the expense, the further ahead you should plan.

4. **Investing:** If you've checked off the basics, you're likely ready to invest. Investing a regular amount monthly will have a big impact long term.

When your financial goals or worries become more complex, invest in a financial plan. Financial planners can help you determine how much is enough to invest while accommodating specific goals like career changes, fertility treatments, or a relocation.

# CHAPTER 6

# Marriage Is a Legal Contract

---

*"You can never know everything, and part of what you know
is always wrong. Perhaps even the most important part.
A portion of wisdom lies in knowing that. A portion of
courage lies in going on anyways."*
—Robert Jordan, Winter's Heart

WHEW. We just covered all the important basics of premarital financial planning. That might feel like a lot. It should, honestly. Figuring out how to merge your finances with intention and making sure you've got a long-term financial plan in place—those are huge foundational steps for building a future together. What's more, those are the foundational steps to prepare for any potential prenup decisions.

Before we get into whether or not you might want a prenup, let's go over some important concepts and definitions pertaining to marriage, divorce, and property. While you don't need to learn much legalese to get a prenup, this chapter covers the language that will come up as you consider the pros and cons of getting a prenup.

# SOME FACTS ABOUT DIVORCE

Here's a sobering fact you probably already know: Divorce rates are still holding steady at 50%. They have remained this way for a long time now, and I don't anticipate that changing. Our court system is not designed for divorce to be a process that 50% of the American population goes through—so you have to look out for yourself.

The divorce process in the United States is not meant to be easy or transactional. It's really designed as a last resort, and it's often long, drawn-out, expensive, and terribly unpleasant. Divorce does not work like it does in the movies. You can't just hire a cutthroat attorney to be sure you get what you want.

*Anyone who's had a family matter decided in court knows that when your family goes to court, no one wins.*

When you establish a prenup, you are laying down a quality foundation for communication, healthy finances, and expectations that, I hope, really reduces the odds that you ever need a divorce or want one. I want your prenup to help you have a long-lasting, wonderful marriage. My other hope for you is if you do end up getting a divorce someday that, it is not more painful, protracted, or expensive than necessary.

Since America's divorce process is geared toward more of a last-resort situation, any kind of legal process is always messy, usually expensive, and takes longer than it needs to. No one wants that, and a prenuptial agreement is really the only way to be sure you know how your money and assets would be treated in a divorce. It is on you to understand how your district and courts will treat certain types of assets in a divorce.

Even if you really know the laws of your state and how divorce works, or you talk to an attorney who knows it well enough to tell you how your money and assets would be treated in a divorce, all that information is still dependent on your divorce actually going to court. Most divorces actually get mediated or settled before going to court, which I recommend if you ever have to go down that road.

In that case, with your prenup in hand, you'd be able to spell out the majority of how your assets would be treated without much effort. Anything not falling under the provisions of the prenuptial agreement can just be mediated so that you don't have to go to court.

In reality, if you mediate, even though that's the more pleasant, faster, typically less expensive route for a divorce, the laws of your courts become even less relevant. What becomes relevant is what you can agree on.

You can probably see this spoiler alert coming, but if you're getting divorced, you and your soon-to-be ex might not feel the most amicable. Give yourself an edge and ensure you only have to discuss as few items as possible. This is yet another reason why a prenuptial agreement is so valuable. Not only because it can help you create a quality foundation for your relationship, help you manage finances, and assist you in having uncomfortable conversations if you need it for a divorce, but you will have already pre-negotiated enough of the items that need to be dealt with. Anything left over will likely be minor and settled quickly without high expenses.

# HOW DIVORCE WORKS

You should know if you don't get a prenup and get divorced, your state has default laws that will apply to your divorce. To assess whether or not you want a prenuptial agreement, you need a basic understanding of how default divorce laws work.

The default divorce laws pertain to where the splitting couple has residence. It doesn't matter where they got married. Whether you're in a community property state or an equitable distribution state, the basic concepts are the same. Generally, anything considered separate property at the time of divorce belongs to the owner of that property, and anything considered marital (or community) property is split.

# STATE LAWS VARY

Please understand that when I reference "state laws," I am generalizing. I can't possibly cover and be an expert on the laws in all 50 states. No one can. So, please pledge to do your due diligence.

If I give an example of a clause or an asset, for instance, as unprotected by a particular state law, you must know that this may not be the case in some states. This is why attorneys specialize.

I want you to feel equipped to embark on a productive prenup-getting process. You are not going to get there if I bog down this book with legal concepts like coverture formulas and the Uniform Premarital Agreement Act (UPAA). (Look these up if you need to.) I should also add that I honestly don't think you need to get into the weeds at that level to do this whole prenup thing right. You really don't.

Keeping in mind that state laws vary, and you don't know with 100% certainty that you will stay in one state for the rest of your life (because how could you possibly know that?), *that's* reason enough for everyone to get a prenup. The existing divorce process leaves divorcing spouses unprepared and blindsided. No one is prepared properly because no one *can* prepare properly. A prenup is the closest you can get to being an expert on the rules that apply to you.

# SEPARATE PROPERTY

Separate property refers to possessions that are owned by one spouse only. You might also hear them called "non-marital assets." Without a prenup, this generally applies to property acquired before marriage, as well as inheritances and gifts received during marriage. You can override state laws regarding how separate property is defined in your prenup. In fact, that's one of the most common functions of a prenuptial agreement.

Now, this next part is important: Separate property only maintains its special separate property protections if you keep it separate. Doing that is not always as easy as you might think. If possessions are not clearly delineated as separate property, they are considered . . .

# MARITAL PROPERTY/COMMUNITY PROPERTY

I'll primarily use the term "marital property" to describe assets that make up the marital estate. You might also see this listed as "marital assets." These are the assets that would be split between a couple should they divorce. If you live in a community property state, the assets that make up the marital estate are called community property, not marital property, but the concept is the same as it pertains to divorce and asset division.

# EQUITABLE DISTRIBUTION STATES AND COMMUNITY PROPERTY STATES

You can look up whether your state is an equitable distribution state or a community property state. If you're in the former, assets shared by a married couple are called marital property. In the latter, they're called community property. Are there other differences? Yes. Do they matter? Only for certain situations.

There seems to be a lot of noise around these concepts so I'm going to reiterate that, for the purposes of the average couple, you do not need to immerse yourself as to why. For example, Wisconsin laws use the term "marital property," but Wisconsin is often considered a community property state. If you are affected by such a situation, use the information in this book to make informed decisions while preparing for your prenup, and let the pros advise you on your specific situation.

To reiterate…

*Generally, divorces in community property and equitable distribution states work similarly. Separate property is protected as separate, and the marital estate is divided.*

The difference between community property and marital property carries more importance during your marriage than in a potential divorce.

The following chapter covers a number of reasons you might want to consider getting a prenup to override your default state laws. Since we're already on the subject of community property, here's one to get you thinking.

## Community Property During Marriage

If you are in a community property state, all property earned or acquired during marriage—and therefore considered community property—is considered to be owned 50/50 by each spouse. This is the case during the couple's marriage, and this law applies regardless of how said property is actually titled (unless your prenup stipulates otherwise). For example, a business one spouse starts during their marriage that's titled only in their individual name still gives their spouse 50% ownership. In some states (though not all community property states), this law actually gives that spouse voting rights in said business.

If you're in a community property state filing separate taxes, it can still mean each spouse needs to claim 50% of their spouse's income on their tax return. I'm breaking my own rule by diving into some of the messy possibilities here only to make the point that it's worth consulting a professional licensed in your state if you have concerns and are confused about whether you want a prenup. I suggest consulting your accountant about any implications regarding tax filings and, of course, an attorney about any of the laws pertaining to your property rights.

# IMPORTANT DEFINITIONS

## Premarital Assets

These include assets and possessions you owned before marriage.

## Commingling

To commingle assets is to mix separate and marital property. Most often, this is done by literally putting separate property money and marital property money in the same account. This can also look like adding a spouse to a separate property home or investment title.

For example:

1. Income earned during marriage is considered marital property (unless otherwise agreed in your prenup). Let's say you deposit your paycheck earned during your marriage into a premarital

account—an account you owned before marriage. That pre-marital account was likely considered separate property until you started mixing in your marital property funds. i.e., your income.

2. You start an investment account with money inherited from your grandmother. Later, you add your spouse to the account so you can both keep adding funds to invest—this account now becomes a joint account. That inheritance money was likely considered separate property until you changed the title of the account.

## Spousal Support

Spousal Support, also called alimony or spousal maintenance, is the name for ongoing payments one spouse makes to the other following a divorce, usually for a limited period of time. Most often, divorcing couples don't have a prenup with specified spousal support terms, so the amount is set during their divorce either by agreement or by order of the court. Some jurisdictions have fixed formulas for calculating the amount, while others let judges make their own assessment based on factors such as each spouse's income level and the length of the marriage.

Now that you're armed with more of the important knowledge everyone should have before getting married, let's get into what you should consider when deciding if you want to get a prenup and if one is right for you.

# CHAPTER 7

# Do You Need a Prenup?

---

*"Plan for what is difficult while it is easy.*
*Work at what is great while it is small."*
—Laozi, The Daodejing of Laozi,
Translation by Philip J. Ivanhoe

THE INTERNET IS FULL OF REASONS people should get a prenup. Most of those are true, but let's cut to the chase.

The real reason to consider a prenup is to create a stronger sense of safety and, therefore, a stronger sense of partnership in your relationship.

For some people, protecting assets they've worked hard to acquire helps create that sense of security they need. Others want assurance that they will be okay even if their marriage doesn't work out. Field whatever comes up in your prenup discussions; do the gut check and ask yourself: *Will this make me feel more secure in our marriage?* Then, ask your partner what they need to feel more secure. I assure you that you can get to that sense of safety you need separately and as a couple.

Now, let's review some of the more concrete reasons people might consider prenuptial agreements.

Two of the most common situations in which people get prenups are 1) when there is a significant difference in wealth or the amount of wealth or 2) when one partner owns a business. I have dedicated a chapter to these very important topics because there's a lot to consider in each of those situations.

Before we get to those, here are some of the less talked about scenarios when people should contemplate getting a prenup.

# YOU HAVE A BLENDED FAMILY

*Default marital property laws and most state laws are primarily designed to address couples in a first marriage, not blended families.*

How could there be any umbrella laws that fit everyone and their circumstances?

To be fair, some states have estate laws that attempt to address a blended family situation by automatically dividing the first portion of an estate between a spouse and the decedent's children, but not every state does this, and the reality is the odds that any default marital property laws or estate laws fit your wishes are exceedingly low for a couple with a blended family.

For example, it's possible that default state laws will give all of your assets and money to your surviving spouse if that circumstance ever happens. If there is no prenuptial agreement or estate plans to address your wishes, your surviving spouse can effectively disinherit your child.

You automatically need a customized plan if you're getting married and have children from a previous relationship. Cue the prenup! A prenup may set aside funds for your children's future education, spell out who will be responsible for certain expenses during your marriage, and/or protect your future spouse from financial obligations to your children or an ex-spouse.

You can also include estate wishes in your prenup to ensure your estate plan goes into effect as soon as you're married. For example, a prenup can direct that a family home goes to your children after your death. Not only is this a prudent step to take, but it can also ease the minds of your family members when they know you already have an estate plan in place that takes your children and spouse into consideration.

One additional benefit to putting estate plans in a prenup is that both partners have to agree to an amendment if they want to change those plans later. If a couple does not have a prenup and their estate wishes are spelled out only in their wills or in a trust, one spouse can make changes to their estate plan unilaterally.

# YOUR FAMILY RELIES OR WILL RELY ON YOU

If you already support family members and want to be able to continue providing them financial support in the future, you may want to consider a prenup to spell out your expectations. I've run into this with a fiancée who already knew she would be supporting her parents through the end of their lives. She wanted to be sure that she had the option to build up separate property from her income during the course of her marriage so that she could rely on that nest egg for her family even if she got divorced.

# ONE PARTNER HAS MORE DEBT

Debt is among the most challenging aspects of joining finances. Existing debt can become the other partner's responsibility, and debt incurred during the marriage may also be fair game for creditors. Prenuptial agreements can go a long way toward clearing the air, sparking healthy conversations, and setting clear boundaries to help everyone feel protected.

# YOU OWN YOUR HOME

By default, premarital investments are protected as separate property when you get married, even without a prenup. However, this is less cut and dry if that premarital investment is in a home. If you have equity in a home prior to marriage and you're planning to live in that home as a married couple, you are, at best, creating a gray area. Yes, you owned that equity before marriage, but now it's a marital home.

*At worst, you may have completely recharacterized your premarital home equity as marital property by getting married without a prenup to protect that equity.*

This scenario illustrates one of the most obvious cases for a prenup. And remember, your default state laws were intended to let you protect premarital assets as separate property! You're not even asking for anything beyond what the state laws afford people with other types of premarital assets.

**Example:** Ann has $100,000 in equity in the home she bought years before getting engaged. Luke has $100,000 in an investment account. They plan to keep Ann's home and live in it even after they're married. By default, without a prenup, Luke's investments can remain protected as separate property as long as he keeps that account separate from their marital assets. Easy-peasy.

However, Ann's equity in the home *does not* get the same special protections. Some state laws would still consider the value of her premarital home equity to be her separate property, but not all states.

# ONE PARTNER FORGOES PAID WORK

If a couple decides that one partner will put a career on hold to undertake family-oriented duties, a prenup can help protect that partner. This can include annual contributions to an IRA, a life insurance policy, or other financial arrangements that allow the non-working spouse to create wealth on their own terms.

As Certified Divorce Financial Analyst Pam Friedman puts it in her book, *I Now Pronounce You Financially Fit,* "Do not assume that *alimony* (spousal support) is automatic for a stay-at-home spouse. In some states, it's nearly impossible to get anything other than already-limited child support."

Keep in mind there may be factors to consider with regard to unpaid work, even when both partners intend to continue paid work. World-renowned relationship experts Dr. John and Dr. Julie Gottman assert that the one type of work that reliably causes conflict for couples is unpaid work.[12] While we all have to do unpaid work to make life happen, women—whether employed or not—still spend over two hours more of their average day on unpaid work than men.[13]

This sort of unpaid work is certainly a contribution to your marital life and shouldn't be dismissed as irrelevant when negotiating a prenup. While I don't necessarily suggest you include terms in your prenup about household responsibilities, I strongly suggest you remember at all times that everyone has valuable contributions to offer a marriage.

---

12   Gottman, John; Gottman, Julie Schwartz; Abrams, Doug; Abrams, Rachel Carlton. *Eight dates essential conversations for a lifetime of Love.* S.l.: Workman Publishing Company, 2019.

13   "American Time Use Survey 2023." U.S. Bureau of Labor Statistics. Accessed August 24, 2024. https://www.bls.gov/data/.

# HIGH-EARNING WOMEN

Statistically, women still bear the brunt of domestic labor and various types of invisible labor in heterosexual relationships. Sage Journals notes that, after having children, when the woman is also the primary earner, she actually contributes an even higher percent of domestic labor compared to women earning the same as or slightly less than their male partners.[14]

In addition, when women earn *significantly less* and *significantly more* than their husbands, they do more housework than women who earn roughly the same amount of income as their husbands.

I hope this uneven labor distribution will change, but, like everything, it will take time. It's something to consider until we get there as a society. Default state laws are generally designed to assume that two partners have contributed equally throughout their marriage, whether their contributions were monetary or not.

Of all the women I've interviewed who have been divorced, the stories of those who had been the primary earners stand out in my memory the most. The common thread among our conversations was a desperation to save other women from what happened to them. They felt exploited, both in their marriages and by their divorce settlements.

# STOCK COMPENSATION

Equity is increasingly part of employer compensation packages. Employers use this type of compensation to incentivize employees. Employees get to own a bit of the company they're working for. If

---

14   Gendered housework: Spousal relative income . . . Accessed August 24, 2024. https://journals.sagepub.com/doi/10.1177/09500170211069780.

a company goes under, the employee's equity could end up being worthless, but this type of asset also has the potential to suddenly be worth vast amounts of wealth—years after it was originally granted.

# PAST DIVORCE TRAUMA

I've never had to sell a divorced person on the idea of getting a prenup. They've been through a divorce, which means they've had that "oh shit" moment when they realized not only are they about to get divorced (which is painful enough), they are learning how their state's divorce laws work. They've looked at the life they've built, boiled down into a spreadsheet, chopped roughly in half, and thought, *why aren't they teaching us these things before we get married*?!

I've also had clients come to me ready for a prenup purely because they've seen enough divorce around them, and they want a plan in place for their separate and marital assets.

# ADDICTION

If one or both partners have a history of addiction, a prenup can put guardrails in place to give their partner peace of mind.

For instance, a couple came to me in advance of preparing their prenup because the groom had a history of gambling addiction. He even had to file for bankruptcy because of it. When I met with this couple, his gambling was years behind them, and he was just months away from completing his bankruptcy process.

He was still in therapy and said he planned to continue "probably forever." His fiancée had supported him through that very difficult time. She was so proud of him, and she finally felt ready to commit to a marriage with him, but she also wanted the reassurance of knowing that if he struggled with gambling again, she wouldn't be on the hook for any of his secret debts. Sensibly, she also wanted to protect the equity she'd built up in the home she owned.

This couple ultimately decided in their agreement that any separate debts they took out would remain separate, the equity she owned in the home prior to marriage would remain her separate property, and any value they built in the home going forward would be split 70/30. That is also how they split their contributions to the home mortgage and home maintenance costs going forward—as they reasonably expected she would continue to bring in a higher income.

## CLARIFYING FINANCES DURING MARRIAGE

There's a relatively new trend of younger people getting a prenup more to clarify finances than to use it as a reactive concern for a divorce. For a plethora of pragmatic reasons, these couples want a clear plan and boundaries. This is reason enough to get a prenup!

In my first few weeks at Morgan Stanley as a client service rep, I was told everyone in my household was required to hold their assets at Morgan Stanley. I'd only been married two years at that point.

I'd taken this part-time job while finishing up grad school. I had zero ambitions about working in finance long-term. Still, I was supposed to go ask my husband to move away from his lifelong advisor to someone he hadn't even met yet?

I was a bit mortified at the thought. Then, as I sat down at my desk, a lightbulb went off. *But I have a prenup*! I went to the compliance officer and explained that I had a prenup that separated our household assets. They asked me to bring in a copy and that was that. *Phew. Tricky relational dilemma averted.*

# CLEAR IS KIND

Marriage is not always hard, but when you hit a difficult season—and it's rare for a marriage not to—if you can provide clarity, it is helpful.

*This is why I do what I do. I believe I can help couples build stronger relationships and create more safety for them to navigate those difficult seasons.*

I can't tell you how many calls I get from people who ask, "Can you look at my finances and tell me the likely outcome if I get divorced?" They usually haven't filed yet or started divorce proceedings. Some haven't even indicated to their spouse that they are considering divorcing.

What I have learned is that people in these situations, like all of us humans, really dislike uncertainty. The problem is that even if I know their state's laws well, it is impossible to predict how somebody's assets will be split. Even if they're never going to move from their state, *and* I know those laws, there are still variations from district to district. As I mentioned, we also don't know if their case would definitely go to court. If it does, what would a judge say? Or would they end up mediating? How well would they and their attorneys do navigating the mediation process? These are all hypotheticals.

Without a prenup, even if you negotiate a divorce agreement without going to court, your outcome still might not be favorable. It could come down to who's willing to fight harder, who will pay more in attorneys' fees, etc. These variables can put you in a stressful position.

*The clearer you can be, the more you can lower the risk of needing to go to court, the better. This is why I believe everybody should get a prenup.*

Just so you don't think that I am rah-rah prenup, I support the couple who've learned enough to know everything I've just described, as well as a few other facts I share with them at their consult who still think *that's not for us.* I don't have concerns around that. I am motivated to provide education and knowledge about prenups.

# CONSIDERATIONS WHEN BLENDING FAMILIES

If you recently married into or are considering marrying into a beautiful, blended family, congratulations! Use the following topics and questions to help guide you as you think about how you'll merge your families and manage your finances going forward.

## Previous Marriages

- Do either of you have ongoing or unresolved terms in a divorce agreement? Examples:
  - Outstanding asset divisions
  - Assets or debts still in joint name
  - Spousal support obligations or income
- Will remarriage impact your social security benefits?

# Children

- If you have child custody and/or child support to consider, be sure to include the expected timelines in your financial plan. Child support typically ends when a child turns 18 or graduates high school, but do check your specific divorce agreements.

- How do you plan to fund the needs of minor children (e.g., education costs) in a way that feels fair?

> **Note:** Financial aid for FAFSA schools is based primarily on the income and assets of the custodial parent.

- How will you make decisions about gifts and support provided to adult children in a way that feels fair?

Review your insurance coverage to ensure you have a plan to cover the following upon death, if applicable:

- Outstanding obligations
- Children's education
- Debts and liabilities
- Living expenses for anyone dependent on you financially but won't inherit your estate (i.e., spouse or children).

# Family Home vs. Marital Home

- If you plan to leave your home to your children, make sure you have a plan for your spouse. You may even include that plan in your prenup.

- Conversely, if you plan to leave your home to your spouse, make sure there's a plan for your children who may want access to the home or who may have feelings about losing a childhood home.

There are lots of estate strategies you can use for a family home. An attorney can help you make a plan for your home that works for your family.

CHAPTER 8

# Prenups and Asset Protection

---

*"Being smart isn't good enough. You need to be educated, and you need to be open-minded, and you need to remember that what you don't know can most definitely hurt you."*
—Seanan McGuire

TRADITIONALLY, financial advisors and probably most attorneys would tell you to strongly consider a prenuptial agreement if there is a large difference in wealth between the betrothed or if one or both partners own significant and illiquid assets like a business or investment real estate. You might also create a prenup if one of you anticipates receiving a large inheritance, is the beneficiary of a trust, or already has a trust.

Using a prenuptial agreement to predefine how you would treat your income and existing and forthcoming wealth is equally valuable to what will happen in the event of a split.

*Real professionals and people with your best interests at heart would advise you and yours that the aforementioned reasons for establishing a prenuptial agreement are solid.*

But not everyone has your best interests in mind. Be aware that some professionals will think you need a prenuptial agreement to protect the person with the most money. They are obviously living out the stereotype for the reason prenups are misunderstood and misapplied.

This outdated mentality does not match my hope for you. I want you to have clarity and an agreement that you think is fair and appropriate—that will feel good in your relationship.

The goal of a good and healthy prenup is for it not to be an uncomfortable agreement to revisit. Keep that in mind if other professionals, especially attorneys, push you to extremes in building your prenuptial agreement. They should be looking out for you and your best interests. That's their job; it's what they should do.

*It's not their job to care about the quality of your relationship in the future. It just isn't. That's your job. If you think that what you are writing today is going to hurt you or your relationship down the road, don't agree to it.*

You must take in the information any attorney or other professionals share with you about how far you could take a prenuptial agreement to protect your interests. Then it's your job to say, "Okay, thank you for this information, and here is what I actually think is fair." It's your job to confirm the criteria you want to cover. Only by adopting this approach can you and your partner or spouse truly make this your signature agreement.

That said, let's explore why someone should seriously consider a prenuptial agreement based on some of the circumstances more commonly associated with them.

# BUSINESS OWNERSHIP

If you own your business, whether outright or with a partner, including it in a prenup can preserve the value, protect partners, and keep the business from becoming marital property as it grows in value during the marriage. It's not uncommon for operating agreements to require partners to establish prenups for this reason. Without a prenup, owners going through a divorce often must split their share of their business with their ex-spouse. That usually means the business owners are left with a choice of selling their business, buying the ex-spouse out of their share, or taking on a new business partner in the form of an ex-spouse.

> *If you both work in the business, you might not want to treat it as a separate property. The takeaway is to make sure you have clarified the terms of the business so you know what you're dealing with.*

Consider getting a prenup if you have ownership, shares, or any kind of interest in a family business or partnership. If you neglected this area and got a divorce, I'm betting your family would not want shares of their business negotiated in the divorce.

They will probably not be open to transferring ownership to the ex-spouse in the event of a divorce, either. This can happen regardless of how anyone feels about it or what they wish. Address this possibility via a prenuptial agreement.

# INVESTMENT REAL ESTATE

If you own real estate, a prenup is a good idea for largely the same reasons it is for business owners. Investment real estate is, in effect, a business, and it should be afforded the same protection.

One man I interviewed for this book, we'll call him Gary, owned a rental property with a partner and friend, Luis. Gary's ex-wife became an additional part owner, as was decreed in their divorce. Luis was adamant that he did not want to sell the property, and neither he nor Gary had the liquidity to buy Gary's ex-wife out of the partnership, so the three of them continued owning the property together for 10 years.

Gary said, thankfully, that the new arrangement was rather uneventful—he and Luis did all the property management, and they simply sent his ex-wife her cut of the rent checks monthly. He clarified that it did get tricky occasionally when they had to make bigger decisions about repairs or tenant disputes.

# ONE PARTNER HAS SIGNIFICANTLY MORE WEALTH

In my opinion, this scenario is the most important to consider a prenup for, but not for the reason you may think. Traditionally, people assume prenups protect the wealth that someone brings to a marriage, but that's only part of what it does.

As we have discussed in other instances, laws vary from state to state. Default state laws generally allow individuals to protect the wealth they bring to a marriage—so long as that wealth remains separate from the marital estate throughout the marriage.

You don't need a prenup for this as long as you're fine with keeping your premarital money behind a figurative wall during your marriage. Without a prenup, protecting one's wealth requires treating that money as separate. Hoarding money away to maintain its special protections . . . Well, that does not sound like the foundation of a productive partnership to most people. A prenup can actually *create* more room for a couple to *confidently share money.*

> **Note:** When marrying an inheritor (someone who stands to receive significant wealth from family), non-inheriting partners should hire a good attorney early on. You're often outnumbered in these cases—so get some expertise and a knowledgeable advocate on your side. See the guide Advice for the Outlaw at the end of this chapter for more tips.

Now, let's forecast into the future and think about what else you might want protected.

# FAMILY WEALTH, TRUSTS, AND INHERITANCES

A prenup can provide reassurance to a family that has amassed wealth they want to keep in their family. This can be achieved by using it to protect a current inheritance, future inheritance, trust assets, or family business interests.

It's important, however, to be transparent about what the family wishes to protect. You may want your family money to stay in the family, but it also makes sense that a future spouse would want clarity about what is being protected, what the family's expectations are for them as it pertains to finances, and what other aspects of this family wealth might affect them.

For example, the future spouse of a trust beneficiary has a right to understand if they will owe taxes on that trust's income distributions, if the trust's capital gains will also be distributed and taxed to the beneficiary, and if requirements within the trust terms could affect their life choices as it pertains to the marriage.

> **Note:** While an inheritance is protected as separate property in most cases, even without a prenup, some states say any appreciation on an inheritance during the marriage is marital property. That means if you inherit an investment account, the growth of those investments could be marital property in certain states if you don't have a prenup that says otherwise.

There are also a number of things you can do with an inheritance that muddy the waters a bit, i.e., using it to fund marital expenses. A prenup can help you clarify how you two wish to treat appreciation during your marriage, as well as any other particulars that might apply.

# ONE PARTNER HAS MORE; ONE PARTNER MAKES MORE

When one partner has meaningfully more premarital assets while the other partner is likely to earn significantly more earnings during the course of the marriage, who needs the prenup more? Trick question. The answer is . . . it depends. Let's look at the following case study to understand how creating a joint future vision is key to answering the question, "Will a prenup make our vision easier to achieve?"

## An Engaged Couple in Austin, Texas

Matt and Maria are in their thirties and living together in Austin, Texas. Matt recently sold a business he founded and plans to keep working on a second business now that his attention isn't divided between two ventures. Maria is in the last year of her fellowship program to become a cardiologist. The couple plans to move states in a year when Maria completes her board certification.

**Matt:**

**Premarital Assets:** $4 million

**Premarital Liabilities:** $0

**Salary:** $0

**Career Outlook:** Speculative. Entrepreneurship may continue to pay off for him, but it also comes with risks.

**Maria:**

**Premarital Assets:** $0

**Premarital Liabilities:** $300,000 in student loan debt

**Salary:** $70,000

**Career Outlook:** Reliable, high salary. Soon to be making $500,000 or more annually. Student loan debt will be forgiven after 10 years of work for a public hospital as part of the Public Service Loan Forgiveness program.[15]

## Joint Goals:

- They'd like to have children.
- Build marital wealth together.
- Have the option to downshift their careers by their mid-50s.
- Considering traveling/volunteer medical work as part of their career downshift (semi-retirement).

---

15    Federal Student Aid. Accessed June 30, 2024. https://studentaid.gov/manage-loans/forgiveness-cancellation/public-service.

## Prenup Goals:

While Matt has already acquired significant wealth prior to marriage, Maria's highest earning years will take place during their marriage. Additionally, their plans to make work optional so they can travel and pursue alternative careers is primarily driven by a lifelong wish of Matt's. Maria is supportive of this vision, but they also recognize this plan will shorten her career. While Matt would like to protect some of his assets, they would also like to include considerations for Maria in their prenup.

## Prenuptial Plan for Matt and Maria:

- Protect most of Matt's assets as separate initially.
- Matt's premarital assets vest and become marital property gradually over time.
- Create the option for Maria to protect future savings she acquires from wages earned during marriage.

# BE OPEN ABOUT YOUR WISHES

It's perfectly reasonable for a family to want to keep family money in their family. It's also perfectly reasonable for a spouse marrying into that family to want some assurances. It's perfectly reasonable to want to protect a business or portfolio you amassed prior to marriage. It's also perfectly reasonable for a spouse to want peace of mind knowing they'd be alright even if the two of you split. One wish I have for these families and couples is that they could all get more comfortable being open about their true desires.

There are endless ways for a couple to manage their finances. If we can be open about our wishes, we can figure out how to manage our money in a way that creates sufficient safety for everyone. We will also be more comfortable reevaluating our setup as our feelings and circumstances change over time.

# ADVICE FOR THE OUTLAW

Most of the prenup resources out there are written for your wealthy fiancé or fiancée and even for your future in-laws. This little guide, dear Outlaw, is just for you.

The fiancé or fiancée with more resources is already at an advantage. In addition to the fact that they likely acquired more financial knowledge simply by growing up in a wealthier family, they may also have a literal team of built-in supporters in their corner during the prenup process, like family, the family's attorney, accountant, etc. It's easy to feel overwhelmed. You're outnumbered.

## Hire Advocates

Hire a divorce attorney with experience being the reviewing attorney (essentially the opposing attorney) on family wealth prenups.

Long-term, what I want for you is a balanced and harmonious marriage, but you're not going to get there by being a people pleaser in this moment. Right now, what that means is you need a knowledgeable advocate (or advocates) on your team. Bringing in competent professionals will minimize the amount of time you feel adrift. This is a time when it's worth investing in this step.

## Get Clear about Your Wishes

You have valuable contributions to your relationship, no matter your financial circumstances. You also have future interests to protect. Do the work to really get clear about what will provide you some reassurance now about your future. Most people in your shoes tell me,

"I just want to know I'm going to be okay." I get that. I felt the same way. But that's not clear enough for a legal agreement. What does "okay" look like to you? Is it knowing you have a roof over your head? Is it knowing you don't have to move if you have children? Is it knowing you could walk away with your own earnings if you needed to? Or how about knowing you have dedicated funds in your name that only you can access? It might not be reasonable to demand everything on your list, but make it full and specific anyway. Get clear about which items will make you feel the most at ease during your marriage. Those are the ones to prioritize.

## Find Trusted Guides

It didn't take long after we married—I'm talking minutes—before I noticed I had helpful guides in my new family. One great aunt popped up first at our reception to congratulate me and start pointing out some faces and names for me. I'll never forget the sweet feeling of being welcomed into a family by someone I hadn't even met before that day.

You might already have noticed during your engagement who is offering you helpful tips and how-to's in your new family's culture. Even if it isn't an explicit introduction as to how the family manages finances, these resources might be in the form of stories. Take note of the information being offered and who to trust, and take advantage of those little moments by asking relevant questions when a door opens. Adjusting to new family cultures takes time, but it isn't all scary. Savor the beauty in this sweet transition as best you can.

## Communication Is Key

Don't brush off concerns or things that don't feel right. It can be easy to make the mistake of attributing misalignments to a new family culture just being different from what you're used to. But that's you making an assumption.

I worked with one fiancée who was marrying a man from Brazil. She wanted to sort out expense responsibilities before going on a trip but said she was worried about offending him. Based on previous conversations where he'd shared that his culture sees men as the "providers," she was pretty sure he would prefer to skip special excursions on their trip, so he could afford to treat her to most of the activities versus going on more excursions and letting her treat him. But she really wanted to do the excursions! I reminded her that no matter their backgrounds, they should talk through it instead of making assumptions. No one's culture should automatically take precedence over the other.

Always bring your concerns back to your partner. Ask about them, and make sure you two are clear about your agreed-upon approach to money, family, etc. Whatever it is. You're making your own shared culture now.

# CHAPTER 9

# How to Bring up a Prenup

*"Safety is the foundation of all functional relationships. We need more than safety, but if we don't have it, none of the other things matter."*
—Jillian Turecki

WHEN IT COMES TO BRINGING UP THE TOPIC of a prenuptial agreement, timing matters, but so does preparation. The right timing might vary from couple to couple and person to person, as each may be in a different stage of readiness. Regardless of when you decide to broach this subject, one thing is crucial—don't skip pre-planning your discussion.

## COMMIT TO REGULAR MONEY CONVERSATIONS

Before we jump off into the deep end and splash cold water on our partners by suddenly launching into a financial conversation, I want to emphasize the importance of regular money conversations in your relationship once again. Whether that means setting a specific date to discuss managing expenses or long-term financial planning, making money discussions part of your regular routine can significantly ease the process.

*Familiarity breeds comfort. When talking honestly about your money aims becomes a habitual part of your relationship, it's less likely to set off alarm bells, making it easier for both parties to be open to new ideas.*

Allow me to clarify something important before I go any further: Initiating these discussions is not about controlling the outcome or manipulating someone into signing a prenup. Don't assume you know what's best for your partner. Instead, work toward creating an environment where both of you can explore a topic that doesn't get talked about enough.

Don't get serious about the money topic until you understand the concept of the "window of tolerance," as I mentioned earlier. This idea changed how I communicate with my husband, and it can make a significant difference in your discussions.

Recognizing when someone is outside their window of tolerance is crucial—so you can shut down any off-track direction. To refresh, signs may include rapid speech, angry body language, or shallow breathing. You know your partner's signs of discomfort better than anyone. Make note of them. If you see these signs, cut the conversation short, and try again later.

# PREPARING FOR THE CONVERSATION

Here are some ideas about how to start the conversation about using a prenuptial agreement. Remember, your exact words aren't as crucial as the intention behind them. The goal is to create an opening for a candid discussion without triggering unnecessary defenses.

# Early Stage

If you're in the early stages of your relationship or not engaged yet, it's best to introduce the concept of your prenup casually. You might say, "Have you ever thought about whether or not you'd want a prenuptial agreement?" The key is to keep it casual and exploratory. You're not suggesting a particular tactic or announcing a decision; you're merely introducing the idea. In an ideal world, you'll start the conversation and learning process together and make the decision to get a prenup jointly.

# Engaged or Certain You Want a Prenup

If you're already engaged or confident you want a prenup, your approach should be more direct but still open. Start with your "why," as in why it's important to you. Communicate your reasons. Be clear but not forceful. It's essential to communicate your honest motivations. See the scripts resource at the end of this chapter for more specific examples.

# Listen and Stay Curious

No matter how your partner responds, be an active listener. Ask questions and stay curious about their perspective. Listen to their feelings and opinions without judgment. Leave room for any reaction, whether positive, negative, or somewhere in between. Your goal is to understand where they're coming from.

# Create a Safe Space for Learning

Resist assigning meaning to your partner's reaction. Traditionally, prenuptial agreements are stigmatized, and there's a lot of misinformation out there. People may have false impressions. Allow them the space to be offended, curious, or supportive. It's all part of the process.

## Keep It Hypothetical at the Beginning of Your Relationship

Ideally, start money conversations early in your relationship. Bring up the topic when it's still hypothetical. It's easier to explore when the result of the conversation isn't geared toward a decision. Include it alongside other hypothetical discussions like having children or future career plans, then blend in how you'd manage money and finances. Start these discussions when they're not yet decisions.

Remember, people's decisions always make sense to *them*. Even if you disagree with your partner, you can at least appreciate their logic when you consider their background, experiences, and perspective. So, again, stay curious, be patient, and make it a joint project. Creating an environment of safety, openness, and curiosity sets the stage for productive discussions about prenuptial agreements. In the end, it's about learning and growing together.

> *No matter the stage you're in, pre-plan your discussion (have a plan for your plan). Keep your person's guard down so they can welcome new concepts.*

Again, none of what I'm describing is to be done to control the outcome or convince somebody to get a prenup. Don't put yourself in a position of manipulating or thinking you know what somebody else should decide is best for them.

## Other Tips for a Productive Conversation

Your first step is to open up both of your brains to think about what we do not spend enough time talking about—our finances and assets and how best to protect them—especially in the company of our significant other.

Another tip for you is to keep it short. Use the window of tolerance as your gauge.

It's okay if you don't make much progress. I have the type of personality that if I really want to, once I'm interested in something or want my partner to take part in an activity with me, I can bulldoze the process. At least, that was my tendency in the past. Two people rarely have the same appetite when it comes to how much they can take on at once. So, I know the value of being careful and that the best approach you can take in your relationship is to be patient and engage in the conversation at an appropriate pace.

Don't forget to make sure you're both physically comfortable as well. I've been guilty of starting too many conversations while standing in the kitchen. You really do need to physically set the stage, so to speak.

We are all operating to the best of our abilities with our particular skills and experiences. When another person knows that you now know where they're coming from, what their feelings are, and that you actually took the time to understand the background of their perspective, you create a layer of safety that will serve you in future conversations.

When your partner knows they can disagree with you and are being heard, they are less likely to put up their guard. In addition to bringing up why you're interested in considering a prenuptial agreement, it wouldn't hurt to share something about their benefits, especially if your partner is harboring lots of false impressions.

I encourage you to conduct your discussion this way because you don't want someone to feel tricked. You want to start with deeply understanding your partner's perspective. Gauge where you fall on the spectrum of merely considering a prenup to being certain it's a deal-breaker if your partner doesn't want one.

If you learn your partner is vehemently opposed, ask, "Why aren't you interested in at least considering one?" If you are on the other side of the table and reading this book to better understand their pro-prenup stance, work to understand your partner's feelings. Ask them: "Why is this important to you?" Or "Why do you already know that you want one?"

It's a big subject, just as getting engaged is, and it makes sense to have some other conversations around spending the rest of your lives together—along with this one. If you're the one voting for the prenup, voice your feelings.

*If you can't find the words to talk about your pro-prenup stance, try: "I was just too scared to bring it up."*

When I hear that reason, I think *that is certainly understandable from my perspective, and hopefully, it is understandable from your partner's perspective.*

When your partner seems receptive, you might ask: "Would you be open to learning more about prenups with me or learning more to consider if it makes sense for us?"

You can also say something like, "I think learning more might help us see if we could address my concerns."

Learning about prenups and considering what you might want in one or not should be in a safe environment—enabling a joint dynamic.

## What If I'm Still Nervous to Bring It Up?

You're likely nervous to bring up a prenup because you're getting ahead of yourself.

Have you actually talked about how you'll *intentionally* manage your finances as a couple? Start there.

"He buys groceries, and I pay for Netflix and Wi-Fi" does not count!

Get your joint financial plan solid first. Put it in writing. After all, how can you jump to suggesting you draft a Plan B (in the form of a prenup) if you haven't even created Plan A yet?

*I find that couples with a solid Plan A are ready to bring up the prenup.*

For more information and guidance, visit www.kaylindillon.com to learn about additional resources that are helpful for laying the groundwork for difficult conversations.

# SCRIPTS TO BRING UP THE PRENUP

Now and then, we all need a little help finding the right words to make a conversation flow more smoothly. I want your money talk to go as well as possible. Please use these resource scripts to bring up a prenup if you need to. I have outlined various scenarios to give you guidance on specific circumstances.

**A note of caution:** You almost certainly shouldn't use these scripts word-for-word. Instead, pay attention to how these examples use care in how they share the speaker's perspective. Find an equally thoughtful version that resonates with you. Remember, your partner cares about how you feel, too. Keep that good feeling flowing between the two of you with the help of these scripts.

## Modern Woman Script

"I want to talk about a prenup. I have the voices of generations of women who had no financial autonomy whispering in my ear. It's a low hum that follows me everywhere.

"I love you to the ends of the earth. I want to be with you and also know that I have checked all the boxes to be a financially responsible modern woman.

"I also believe we can create a prenup that leaves us both feeling protected, not just me. Can we talk about this idea some more? "

## Family Wealth Script

"I want to have an important conversation with you about something that's been on my mind as we plan for our future together.

"My family has always emphasized the importance of protecting our assets. They've strongly encouraged me to get a prenuptial agreement. Beyond their concerns, it's also important to me personally.

"I'm hoping we can consider this idea together as part of a larger discussion around how we plan to manage our finances together as a couple.

"Would you be open to having a conversation about how we might approach this together?"

## Blended Family Script

"I've been thinking a lot about our future together. As we merge our families, I'd like to consider getting a prenuptial agreement.

"I learned that it can be important for blended families to consider one because default laws wouldn't leave us ways to keep certain assets protected for our children as I'm sure we both want to do. I also really like the idea of using a prenup as a tool for helping us clarify how we'll handle our finances during our marriage.

"I didn't have any of these tough conversations before my first marriage, and money was an issue that only festered more over the years. I'd love to start our new life together right, feeling confident we're coming from the same place.

"What do you think?"

## Past Divorce Trauma Script

"I have a big question. Would you be open to considering a prenuptial agreement with me? I know that might sound out of left field, but let me walk you through my thinking.

"As I think about our marriage, I want to be sure we're starting out on the right foot and sorting through important topics that will set us up for success.

"As you know, my parents' divorce was brutal. I believe having clear agreements in place would not only be good for our relationship, but it would also help calm the worried voice in the back of my head that keeps saying, 'Whatever you do, you can never go through that again.'

"I've heard of couples getting pretty plain vanilla prenups that aren't even that different from default state laws, purely because it's a pragmatic step to take before marriage.

"What are your thoughts?"

# CHAPTER 10

# Preparing for Your Prenup

*"I truly believe that a prenup properly shepherded is an enhancement to communication."*
—L. Paul Hood, Jr., JD, LL.M.

IF YOU'VE DECIDED to get a prenup, it's time to prepare. No, don't jump to calling an attorney. Part of why prenups get a bad rap is because most people do them wrong. Most start with the attorney phone call, and they're off to the races. Some couples bumble through the process and end up relatively unscathed. Some fight through it, and real damage is done.

The unscathed ones got lucky. But you don't need luck. You're going to prepare. So, what's next?

## DEFINE YOUR GOALS

Agreeing on your prenup goals before starting that first draft is important. Have I mentioned that enough times yet? Here are some high-level goals to discuss with your partner and consider:

- Protecting existing assets
- Protection from existing debt

103

- Minimizing cost/simplifying any potential divorce
- Behavior incentives/disincentives
- Blended family considerations
- Estate planning considerations
- Non-financial contributions (i.e., family care)
- Business ownership considerations

# FINANCIAL DISCLOSURE

- Share all your financial data:

  1. Income statements:

     This could include pay stubs, W-2s, or statements for pensions, stock options, restricted stock grants, and company benefit plans.

  2. Recent tax returns:

     Include your personal tax returns along with tax returns for trusts, partnerships, or businesses you own or benefit from.

  3. Credit reports

  4. Assets and debt:

     I suggest sharing actual statements for all your assets and debt, including those for trusts or businesses you have interests in. You will also need to provide a summary of this information to your attorney for your prenup disclosure. See the financial schedule template at the end of this section for an example.

> **Note:** If you have a business or private investment, you may need to get a professional valuation in lieu of a monthly statement.

# FINANCIAL SCHEDULE TEMPLATE FOR YOUR PRENUP DISCLOSURES

## Financial Schedule

### Assets

**Cash**

| | |
|---|---|
| Checking Account | $0 |
| Savings Account | $0 |
| Money Market Account | $0 |
| CDs | $0 |
| Life Insurance Cash Value | $0 |
| *Total Cash* | *$0* |

**Invested Assets**

| | |
|---|---|
| Taxable Investment Account | $0 |
| Employer Retirement Account | $0 |
| Health Savings Account | $0 |
| Pension | $0 |
| Annuity | $0 |
| Traditional IRA | $0 |
| Roth IRA | $0 |
| Other Investment Account | $0 |
| *Total Invested Assets* | *$0* |

**Other Assets**

| | |
|---|---|
| Personal Home | $0 |
| Real Estate Property | $0 |
| Business Ownership Interests | $0 |
| *Total Lifestyle Assets* | *$0* |

**Lifestyle Assets**

| | |
|---|---|
| Vehicle | $0 |
| Art & Collectibles | $0 |
| Jewelry | $0 |
| *Total Lifestyle Assets* | *$0* |

*Total Assets* — *$0*

### Liabilities

| | |
|---|---|
| Credit Card Balance | $0 |
| Student Loans | $0 |
| Mortgage | $0 |
| Other Liabilities | $0 |
| *Total Liabilities* | *$0* |

**Total Net Worth** — **$0**

You'll each need to prepare a financial schedule for your prenuptial agreement disclosures. Some attorneys have their own template to use after you provide your financial data. You can use this template to help you get all your information together.

# HOW TO GET A PRENUP

Setting up your prenup can range from a simple process to a rather complex one, depending on your situation. A couple entering a first marriage with relatively comparable wealth and income can have a simple and speedy process. On the most complex end are couples with international law considerations and significant wealth in businesses or private investments that are difficult to value.

Let's review what you can expect during the process.

## Yes, You Need to Hire Attorneys

You will want to hire separate attorneys to help you through the process of working on your prenup and finalizing it. I know, I know. That sounds awful, doesn't it? That's why I wrote this book.

You know what sounds worse than hiring separate attorneys? Entering a legal agreement without a clear understanding of how it affects you. (P.S. That's what most people do when they forgo a prenup . . . enter a legal agreement they don't fully understand.) So, yes, you will want to hire separate attorneys to create your prenup.

A drafting attorney will draft your prenup. The reviewing attorney will review it. Since each attorney represents just one of you, you won't be able to have discussions with your attorney as a couple. You will need to decide which one of you will hire the drafting attorney and which will hire the reviewing attorney. As I noted, the drafting attorney fee will likely be higher than that of the reviewing attorney.

I asked estate planning attorney L. Paul Hood, Jr. for his advice for couples trying to find the right attorney for their prenup. Hood has authored many books and textbooks on the subjects of estate planning and prenuptial agreements. He said, "It's honestly a matter of feeling."

Be sure to interview your potential attorney(s) and get a feel for how they operate and their philosophy on prenuptial agreements. As Hood added, "It's all about the attitude of the representative because if they make the prenup a zero-sum game—like a lot of them do—you might actually kill that nascent relationship."

Reminder: It is your attorney's job to advocate for your individual interests. This is a good thing. It's up to you and your partner to communicate openly and agree wholeheartedly on your final terms. If you use an online prenup service—I'll get to that in a bit—you'll still want to hire attorneys to review the prenup.

## Specialists

Depending on your situation, you may want to consider hiring specific professionals to help you through the prenup prep and drafting process. I've already anticipated that you'll still be wondering which route is right for you, so I created a visual chart showing which professionals and specialists can help you at differing stages of the prenup process. You can find the chart at the end of this chapter.

Here is how different specialists can help you ….

# PRENUP COACH

As discussed earlier, a prenup coach can help you prepare for your prenup together. It's advantageous because an attorney can only represent one partner during this process. Working with a prenup coach ensures you have a guide who can support both of you as needed.

The prenup coach will also help you prepare a plain-language list of goals to take to the drafting attorney for your prenup.

As of the writing of this chapter, I believe I'm the only prenup coach out there, but I also believe a good financial planner knowledgeable in your state's marital property laws can do a great job preparing you for your prenup. We financial planners are great at helping couples get clear about their goals.

# MEDIATOR

If you're concerned about hiring separate attorneys, you can hire a family law mediator. When an attorney mediates a prenup, they can meet with both partners to discuss prenup plans.

Some mediation services prepare a term list—the terms the couple wants in their prenup, similar to a goals list I create with clients. When you work with an attorney mediator, your term list might have the names of clause types included in your initial agreement, which you'll then take to a drafting attorney. Some mediation services will completely draft the agreement for you. The difference between a term list from an attorney mediator and a goal list from a prenup coach is all in the legal specificity. The term list developed with the mediator can be prescriptive for your drafting attorney. In either case, you'll still want your own attorneys to review the agreement.

When you're going this route, you will ultimately hire three attorneys. One is for mediation, one is for you, and one is for your partner. This is a more expensive route but a good option if you believe your situation has the potential to become contentious or your case has enough legal complexity to need a neutral third party with legal expertise.

Even if you don't want to go through the mediation process, you can still hire an attorney who does mediation work to represent you individually. Mediators tend to be great options because they're already focused on helping keep clients out of court.

# FAMILY LAW AND ESTATE PLANNING ATTORNEYS

Generally, I suggest hiring a family law attorney to draft your prenup. More specifically, I suggest hiring a divorce attorney (divorce falls under the legal umbrella of family law).

I know.

You thought it sounded bad enough that you have to hire two opposing attorneys, but now I'm suggesting divorce attorneys at that.

Why?

You want your prenup to hold up, and divorce attorneys work in close proximity to the latest prenup case law.

Alternatively, it might also make sense to hire an estate planning attorney, particularly if you are blending families. If you're curious about which approach is best for your situation, interview attorney options in both specialties and ask them for their input based on your circumstances.

## Collaborative Family Law Attorneys

Collaborative family law attorneys are trained in the practice of collaborative family law—as their title suggests. This is a type of alternative dispute resolution used primarily in divorce cases. During a divorce, going the collaborative route is a middle step between mediation and litigation.

According to the collaborative approach, clients agree upfront not to litigate their matter in court. Instead, each partner hires a collaborative law attorney, and the partners and their attorneys meet only in group sessions. This can help reduce confusion and tension and cut back on back-and-forth between attorneys.

Most collaborative family law attorneys I've encountered are still happy to help with prenups the traditional way, too, AKA without group meetings. So, it's important to be clear upfront about which approach you prefer. I tell my couples that searching for a collaborative family law attorney can be a great way to narrow in on attorneys who aren't going to intentionally stoke fires but will still go the traditional route and meet separately. I prefer for everyone to have an opportunity to get counseled privately by their attorney. Ask all the scary questions you wouldn't normally ask, then go finalize your prenup with eyes wide open.

> **Note:** The group meetings included in the collaborative route are not legal in all states. If you hire collaborative law attorneys and meet separately, the cost will be in line with the traditional route.

# OTHER PROFESSIONALS YOU MAY NEED

You might also need to hire specialists like a real estate appraiser, business valuation expert, or accountant to help with your specific prenup process. A coach or mediator can help you assess upfront which professionals you might need to hire. They've also likely worked with these professionals in the past and can help you search for them if needed.

# Cost

A good rule of thumb concerning the amount of money you may spend is to expect the combined total cost of creating a prenup to be one to two times the typical cost for basic estate documents in any given area. This is in addition to any fees associated with hiring specialists, if applicable. This assumes the couple is clear about their prenup goals before the drafting process and has little back-and-forth. Here in Lawrence, Kansas, that means you can get a prenup done for $1,000 each. In New York City or San Francisco, you're looking at more like $4,000 per person. The cost of the drafting attorney fee will likely be slightly above this estimate, and the cost for the reviewing attorney will likely be slightly below this estimate.

Let's talk about fee types. Some attorneys charge flat fees for prenups, while most attorneys charge hourly fees. In both cases, I tend to see the costs in the same range. If your attorney charges hourly, ask for a rough estimate of the total cost. In my experience, those upfront estimates have come in pretty darn close to the final cost. When I help couples with their attorney search, I'll ask the attorneys on their search list to provide us with estimates. I don't have any data to support this hunch but I suspect that when your financial planner gets the cost estimate for you in advance, attorneys are pretty committed to staying in that range for you. If they didn't stay in the range or communicate well about a change in expectations, they'd certainly fall off my recommendation list quickly.

> **Note:** You can include terms in your prenup regarding who will be responsible for the attorney fees. Some couples want to pay their own attorney, sometimes the individual who originally asked for the prenup ends up paying both attorneys (or reimbursing their partner for their fees), and sometimes couples agree to even out their costs by having the partner with the lower attorney fee reimburse their partner for a portion of their higher attorney fee.

# CAN I DIY MY PRENUP?

As of the writing of this chapter, one thing is clear: IF there's a chance you could DIY your prenup and trust it would hold up, it's only by using HelloPrenup. Full disclosure: I have an affiliate link for promoting HelloPrenup at www.kaylindillon.com, but I still believe this is the best tool to use, so I would recommend it regardless.

I have reviewed all the online prenup options extensively, even signing up and pretending I was getting married all over again, and HelloPrenup is superior. (Unsubscribing from all those reminders to complete my prenup was very annoying, by the way.)

Here's what I like and appreciate about HelloPrenup:

- All their research is right there on the website. It's a great resource whether you use the service or not.
- It's clear on their state pages if an attorney review will be required after completing the online prenup. Some states are rigid about this requirement; some are more flexible. I adamantly recommend that you include an attorney review in either case.
- If you use their service, you can access a menu of attorneys willing to review HelloPrenup prenups for you. (This is pretty huge. Trust me—you can't just take an online prenup to any attorney and ask them to review it!)
- The clauses for each state were written by reputable family law attorneys in that state.

Another bonus to using HelloPrenup is that they do a good job walking a couple through many of the important premarital money conversation topics.

The three main questions I get from people wondering why they need an attorney are: 1) "Why do I need to hire a divorce attorney when we already agree on everything?" 2) "Isn't there a better way to do this, as lawyers are so slow?" and 3) "Why is it so cost-prohibitive?"

Here's Julia Rodger's (CEO and founder of HelloPrenup) take on it:

"So, when you hire an attorney, let's say you and your fiancé each have attorneys; one attorney will put together the draft of the prenup. And then they will give that draft to either the other party—the other fiancé or the other lawyer. The reason that is problematic is that one party is always being presented with a fully completed draft. And so, they always feel like they are in a less advantageous position because they are reacting to the information they have received.

"I designed the [HelloPrenup] platform to be a dual participation system. Both parties complete their part of the questionnaire before there's ever a draft; they walk through the negotiation stage/section before there's ever a draft. And then, they output an agreement containing information they both want."

In one of our conversations about the process, Julia shared what I have found to be true, as well—she finds that many attorneys who draft prenups are family law attorneys; more specifically, they're often divorce attorneys. They tend to operate from a space of "Let's go at this and get the best deal we can" without considering that the parties are getting married. This is the opposite of what they want—a kind of harmonious, happy relationship and an agreement reflecting it's not about winning. It's about finding further clarity within your financial plan.

# REMEMBER, PRENUPS ARE PERSONAL

The prenup process brings with it expectations from both parties and from family and friends—which may or may not be accurate.

I've outlined a list for you to refer to, which can give you a better idea of what is to come. As you read this list, remember to plan for these possibilities

- Dealing with potential reactions or opinions from family members and friends.
- Setting boundaries and making decisions based on you and your partner's needs and goals.
- Recognizing that each couple's situation is unique and personal to them and ensuring needs and wants are heard and represented in the prenup.

# WAYS TO GET A PRENUP

Is your head spinning with all of these prenup options? Here's a visual chart of the best options (in my opinion) that you can also find at www.kaylindillon.com. If you're ready for more guidance, I also offer a course that you can sign up for here, and it includes this chart. Understand, all the ways to get a prenup listed here still involve hiring attorneys.

| | Step 1<br>Make a Money Plan | Step 2<br>Prepare | Step 3<br>Draft & Review |
|---|---|---|---|
| What's Involved? → | Plan for splitting expenses, long-term goals, insurance and tax decisions | Learn about laws & prenups. Discuss goals. Research attorney choices. Prepare financial disclosures. | Interview attorneys & hire. Partner 1 hires drafting attorney. Partner 2 hires reviewing attorney. Draft & finalize prenup. |
| Mediation Route → $$$$ | Financial Planner | Family Law Mediator<br>*Allows you to meet with a knowledgeable attorney and draft the prenup together.* | Family Law Attorney<br>*You each hire one to review your draft.* |
| Traditional Route → $$$ | Financial Planner | Financial Planner knowledgeable in prenups<br>OR<br>The Prenup Coach® | Family Law Attorney<br>*You each hire one* |
| Collaborative Route → $$ | Financial Planner | Financial Planner knowledgeable in prenups<br>OR<br>The Prenup Coach® | Collaborative Family Law Attorney<br>*You each hire one. Meet in group sessions.* |
| DIY Alternatives → $ | *Prenup Partnership* the book<br>OR<br>Couples Money Kit<br>*(Lesson 1&2 of the Prenup Course)* | *Prenup Partnership* the book<br>Prenup Prep Course.<br>OR<br>Hello Prenup | Hello Prenup<br>Hire **Hello Prenup approved attorney** to review your Hello Prenup draft. |

# CHAPTER 11

# Prenup Basics

---

*"Nothing is black or white."*
—Nelson Mandela

AS I WAS WRITING THIS BOOK, I kept asking myself, *what do I wish I'd known when I got my prenup?*

One of the hardest parts about creating this guide is that I really would have liked a clear list of rules and options for prenuptial agreements back when I was getting one. The reality, however, is that legal matters are not so black-and-white. Context matters. Your particular state matters. Without knowing every detail of your situation, the answer to so many questions is "It depends."

This is why no guide can ever replace the importance of getting personalized advice from a licensed attorney.

With that in mind, let's talk rules anyway.

Prenuptial agreements are contracts. The rules governing them are similar to other types of contract law. Like other contracts, prenups range widely from rather basic to very creative.

There are also differences from one state to another in the rules governing prenuptial agreements, so be sure to always consult a reputable family law attorney in your state to confirm your prenup is in good standing. The general concepts here will help you prepare thoroughly first.

# LEGAL CONSIDERATIONS AND REQUIREMENTS

For a prenuptial agreement to be enforceable, you generally need to meet the following requirements:

- Both parties have honestly disclosed their assets and debt. Some states let you waive this, but remember . . . transparency is key to crafting an agreement you will both love.

- Both parties signed the agreement voluntarily.

- Both parties were at least given the time and option to consult an attorney. In some states, separate legal representation is explicitly required. In every state, your attorney will likely recommend this regardless, as do I. Waiving representation comes with certain requirements.

- No illegal or unconscionable terms. Suffice it to say the bar for unconscionable is low. So low that I suggest you assume there are no loopholes down the road. Only sign your agreement if you expect that it will hold up.

If you're like me, you might feel that the language professional people on your team use concerning rules is annoyingly vague. We're talking about rules—so why aren't they concrete?!

Well, it's largely because each state has general laws in place, and how they're interpreted is determined by the case law in that state. That means two important things:

- How one judge interprets a law can have nuanced differences from the interpretations of other judges.

- Case law is always changing because new cases are always coming up.

It would be great if we had one very solid resource for couples nationwide to reference, but the reality is that any such resource would be inadequate and would potentially be outdated as new cases come to light.

The good news is you don't need to be responsible for studying these nuanced differences. You can focus on your main goals. Get a general idea of what's possible with a prenup, then leave the rest to the pros. Now, let's look at what prenups can and can't do.

# PRENUPS *CAN*:

- Set rules for dividing premarital assets or debt in the event of divorce.
- Set rules for dividing assets or debt you accumulate during the marriage in the event of a divorce.
- Allow for future changes.
- Include estate provisions similar to those in a will.
- Set requirements during the marriage.
- Establish rights to a pet or other property.

# PRENUPS *CANNOT*:

- Determine child custody.
- Set child support.
- Incentivize divorce or illegal acts

# DOES BREAKING A RULE GET A PRENUP THROWN OUT?

No. A well-written prenup will include a severability clause that prevents a court from tossing out the entire agreement if one clause is found to be unenforceable.

# BEHAVIOR CLAUSES

Some states disallow behavior clauses like infidelity clauses, and some allow them. You might also hear them called "lifestyle provisions." I'm not a fan of these for the primary reason that even if a particular behavior-related clause is permissible in your state, enforcing these clauses often requires litigation. What's the point of putting all this work into an agreement that might still land you in court if you need to use it? No, thank you.

These next few sections will cover prenup considerations.

*This is not a legal guide. That's what your attorney is for. This is a guide to prepare you for a legal process. I'm including types of terms and considerations to offer you some familiarity with the legal process.*

It's more important for you to be able to clearly communicate your wishes in plain language than it is for you to learn new legal terminology. After all, you don't want to use the wrong term or misuse a term. Neither do I. Lucky for us, we don't have to write the document!

I've seen 3-page prenups, and I've seen 40-page prenups. I've heard lore of even longer prenups. This is one of those areas of life where the last thing you need to do is look around at what someone else is doing as your model. Throw the comparisons out the window and focus on what's right for you.

The term categories in this book are not all-encompassing. Contract law, AKA prenups, can be very creative, as I've mentioned a few times.

What I have included here is meant to help you start envisioning what matters to you and your partner, so you have a solid starting point before you begin your first draft. That is the key to a productive drafting process.

# WHAT STATE MATTERS FOR MY PRENUP?

When you draft your prenup the laws of your state of residence will govern your prenup. So, you'll want to hire an attorney licensed in your state. It does not matter where you get married. If you have residence in one state and plan to move states immediately after you marry, consult attorneys in each state so you can compare the governing laws and choose the one that best supports your prenup goals. In this case, you'll include a "choice of law" clause in your prenup.

# EVALUATING YOUR PRENUP TERMS

As you work on your plans for your prenup, keep coming back to these important questions.

- Does this plan feel fair?
- Does it address the reasons we wanted our terms in the prenup to begin with?
- Will it make managing our finances during marriage simpler or more complicated? If more complicated, is the tradeoff worth it?

- Does it leave enough flexibility for life changes? If not, what's our plan if this doesn't fit well with our situation anymore?

# QUESTIONS TO ASK AN ATTORNEY

I always suggest each partner have their own counsel. Most states require this anyway. The ideal route is for you to be really clear on each of your prenup goals in advance before engaging attorneys.

Concerning the area of law practiced, ask:

- Are you a family law attorney?
- Do you practice collaborative law? If so, do you require that prenups be discussed in group meetings? Or are group meetings allowed in our state?

Regarding their experience, ask:

- How many prenups have you drafted?
- Do you have experience with a prenup being challenged in court?
- What are your tips for minimizing back-and-forth between attorneys during this process?

In queries concerning cost, ask

- How do you charge for prenup services?
- What do you estimate the total cost will be?
- How do you charge for additional draft edits, if needed?

In defining their process, ask:

- What is your process for prenups like?
- Can I give you permission to talk to my advisor regarding my financial disclosures?
- Can you recommend a reviewing attorney you've worked well with before?
- Ask your potential attorney if you can execute documents remotely in your state. Some states and firms allow this. Some do not. If your state does, widen your attorney search area to anywhere in your state. If you are able to do this, it can help you cut costs.

> **Note:** If you are in a high cost-of-living area, search for attorneys in lower cost-of-living areas in your state.

These questions are designed to help you understand the process *before* you hire an attorney. Depending on your wishes, your goal is not necessarily a "yes" to each one. Do not hire an attorney who you feel has not given you the answers you are looking for. It's okay to shop around for a little while. Getting a prenup is an important milestone in your relationship. The person you trust most to do the lion's share of lifting on your legal team should inspire feelings of confidence in you. If they don't, move on until you find someone who does.

# CHAPTER 12

# Prenup Terms You Need to Know

---

*"If you stay ready, you won't have to get ready."*
—Sauce Brady

I THINK THAT QUOTE SAYS IT BEST. You have come this far in the book to learn how to be best prepared to begin this process; that includes learning the applicable terms that apply to the prenup-getting process. Your attorney might call these "provisions" or "clauses." Simply put, these are topic areas you can address in a prenup.

You might be tempted to look at these lists as menu items. Resist that urge. Stay focused on your primary goals for getting a prenup, and let your goals guide you, whether the items on these lists are in line with your agreed-upon vision or not.

# PRENUP TERMS RELATED TO ASSET DIVISION AT DIVORCE

## Premarital Assets and Debt

Your prenup can clarify that you want your premarital assets to be treated as separate property. While this is generally how states already classify premarital assets, putting it in a prenup can firm up how you define your separate property and help you avoid gray areas. A prenup can also spell out ways you wish to be more generous with premarital assets than your state laws allow, as some case studies mentioned previously have illustrated.

## Post-Marital Assets and Debt

A prenup can specify which assets acquired during the marriage should be considered marital property and which should be considered separate property. While default state laws generally say all post-marital assets and debts are marital property, your prenup can divert from this definition. For example, a prenup can specify that each person's earnings during marriage are their own separate property. Or that any debts taken out in an individual's name only are that individual's separate debts.

> **Note:** The Employee Retirement Income Security Act (ERISA) only allows spouses to waive their right to a spouse's qualified retirement plan after they are married.[16]

If you desire to keep your 401k separate, you may need to address this after you are married. If this is your wish, discuss your options with your attorney.

## Personal Residence

Including a marital home in a prenup comes with a lot to consider. For that reason, I've given this topic its own chapter. Lots more on this coming up soon . . .

---

16    Hood, L. Paul. *Yours, Mine & Ours: Estate Planning for People in Blended or Stepfamilies (Planning Your Future).* Mount Pleasant, SC: Bublish, Incorporated, 2022.

## Engagement and Wedding Rings

In case you're wondering, an engagement ring is considered a completed gift made prior to marriage, and in most states, it's the separate property of the person receiving the ring. Premarital assets are generally considered separate property even without a prenup. But your prenup can specify whether you want your engagement and wedding rings defined as marital or separate property. This is a particularly good idea if any of the jewelry pieces are family heirlooms that you want to be sure stay in your family.

## Lump Sum Payment

Another optional addition to your prenup is the lump sum payment clause. It stipulates if you were to divorce after having been married for a certain period of time, or during which you hit specific milestones, then one party will pay the other an exact amount of money.

In cases where women choose to leave their professions to raise children and are subjected to a wealth gap that they won't necessarily be able to make up by going back to work, this clause can be considered.

## Spousal Support

Also referred to as alimony or spousal maintenance, spousal support is an ongoing payment made to a spouse after divorce. Your prenup can predetermine a potential spousal maintenance amount, set a formula for calculating that amount in the future, or waive the right to collect spousal support should you divorce. In most states, the rules for writing an enforceable prenup are even stricter if you include a waiver of spousal support in your prenup. A lawyer can help you weigh the pros and cons of including terms around spousal support.

**Note:** You can also include terms requiring one spouse to provide the other with health insurance following a divorce.

# PRENUP TERMS RELATED TO LIFE DURING MARRIAGE

Prenup clauses that affect your life during marriage should still be financial in nature to be enforceable. Yes, you can use your prenup to spell out who will do the dishes if there's a financial component to that requirement! But I don't recommend it. See Behavior Clauses in Chapter 11.

## Set Responsibility for Expenses

Your prenup can set rules that govern who will be responsible for certain expenses.

In this instance, a prenup can:

- Require a partner with significant premarital assets to be responsible for the income taxes resulting from their investments or for all of the couple's tax burden. Consider each partner's premarital tax bracket as part of the exercise of determining what's fair for you two.

- Require a partner with a child or children from a previous relationship to be separately responsible for certain expenses, like college tuition, for example.

- Stipulate that a partner protecting a certain separate property, like a home, is solely responsible for the maintenance costs for that property.

# Life Insurance Requirement

Your prenup can require one or both partners to maintain a certain amount of life insurance coverage for the benefit of the surviving spouse. This is a good idea for beneficiaries of a family trust or business whose assets wouldn't go to their spouse in the event of their death. It's also a good idea if you have a blended family, and a significant portion of one spouse's assets will go to their children upon their death instead of to their spouse.

# Income and Account Types

Your prenup can set rules for what account types you'll have and where income will be deposited. As a financial planner, I feel compelled to say: Please don't set these rules unless you have a clear reason for doing so.

You'll likely want flexibility during your marriage to determine the right approach for yourselves at different stages. Nonetheless, setting certain specifics could make sense if you already know one spouse won't be working outside the home. Requiring that income be deposited into a joint account only could ensure the non-working spouse has equal access to the shared marital resources. You could even stipulate that a portion of income be deposited into an account only the stay-at-home parent controls, ensuring that this spouse always maintains as much financial autonomy as their working spouse.

# Gifts During Marriage

Your prenup can require a spouse with significant premarital wealth to make gifts to their spouse at certain intervals.

For example, a partner protecting millions as separate property under the prenup could agree to gift $50,000 or another set amount to the marital estate each year, thus building up a corpus of shared wealth that will grow over the course of the marriage.

Gifts can also be characterized under the prenup as separate property of the receiving spouse, thus allowing the spouse the opportunity to build up their own separate property.

# PRENUP TERMS RELATED TO EVERYTHING ELSE

## Estate Clauses

Most prenups will include a clause that declares whether the prenup's definition of separate property waives the inheritance rights of a surviving spouse. In other words, the prenup will say whether the separate property named in the prenup should also be treated separately as part of the deceased spouse's estate or if the surviving spouse would have a legal claim to it.

Some prenups will include even more estate-related terms than this. A prenup can spell out exactly how each spouse wants their assets dispersed at death, just as one would in a will or trust.

Clear as mud?

This is why I stick with plain language goals. What do you want to happen to your assets when you die? Do you want the option to change that in your will at any time, or do you want it in your prenup?

# Reputation, Confidentiality, and Non-Compete Clauses

These are complicated topics, so briefly, just know that you can set rules around these subjects, which may make sense for some. Regardless of what you include, allegations that these clause(s) were violated will need to be reviewed by a judge.

# Sunset Clause

A sunset clause means your prenup will expire on a certain date or anniversary, depending on what you choose.

The benefit of this type of clause is that you can write in some protections for separate property in the case you aren't married very long, but after a certain point in time, say, after you've been married for many years, that distinction can go away.

The downside of such a clause is that if your marriage hits a tough season, an impending sunset clause can feel like a deadline to make a decision. James Sexton, New York City divorce attorney and author of *If You're In My Office, It's Already Too Late,* cites sunset clauses as a cause for increased divorce rates as couples near that sunset deadline.

I couldn't find reliable data to back this up, but that doesn't mean you shouldn't think about it. Every marriage will have difficult times. If you're experiencing one, you might not want the added pressure of a looming sunset date when your financial agreement will change.

On the flip side, if your primary concern is about splitting assets following a very short marriage and you're less concerned about a split after a long and hard-fought marriage, perhaps a sunset clause is exactly what you want. It's worth noting, however, that most states take the length of a marriage into account during a divorce split, even when the couple has no prenup.

# Fertility

If you've gone through the process of freezing eggs for a future family, you can include terms around who will have rights to those eggs if you divorce. If you anticipate going through this process in the future, you can also include terms around those rights. Please note: Embryos cannot be in a prenup.

# Pet Rights Clause

A pet clause allows couples to decide what happens to their pet(s) in the event of a divorce. Usually, this means predetermining who would have rights to a pet, but less commonly, this can mean spelling out ground rules for jointly caring for a pet following a divorce.

# Counseling and Mediation

A prenup can include an agreement to try counseling or therapy before resorting to a divorce filing. Additionally, you can include terms in your prenup that stipulate you will try to mediate your divorce, should you go that route, prior to resorting to a court proceeding.

*As is the case with everything in this book, consult your attorney to ensure your plan complies with your state's laws.*

I hope the options in this chapter provide a starting point for your discussions on what you might want to include in your prenup. It is crucial to communicate openly, work to understand each other's perspectives, and achieve a mutually beneficial agreement reflective of your joint financial contributions.

# PRENUP PREP CHECKLIST

Start with this prenup prep checklist as a guide for the types of items you can address in your prenup. Complete this checklist with your partner before hiring attorneys. Then, provide a copy to each of your attorneys to be sure your first draft meets your goals.

Working collaboratively to come to a mutual position with the items on your list is the key to a positive prenup drafting experience.

## Sample Prenup Prep Checklist

Names:

Wedding Date:

To-Do's

- ☐ Prepare financial schedules for your prenup disclosures.
- ☐ Define your goal(s) for your prenup. (*See Prenup Goals below.*)
- ☐ Discuss what items you want to address in your prenup. (*See Items to Consider section below.*)
- ☐ Hire attorneys.

## Prenup Goals

- ☐ Protect existing assets.
- ☐ Protection from existing debt.
- ☐ Minimize cost/simplify any potential divorce.
- ☐ Behavior incentives/disincentives.
- ☐ Blended family considerations.
- ☐ Estate planning considerations.
- ☐ Consider non-financial contributions (i.e., family care).

☐ Business ownership considerations.

☐ Custom:

☐ Custom: <u>Items to Consider</u>

**Goal:** Get on the same page at a conceptual level. Your attorney will recommend the best way to address your wishes. Prioritize the bolded items in particular. Not all items will apply to you. Talking to your partner in advance is key. Your attorney will help you decide what to include.

| **Premarital Assets** | **Separate** | **Marital** | **Custom Note** | **Seeking Attorney Guidance** |
|---|---|---|---|---|
| Investments | ☐ | ☐ | | ☐ |
| Property | ☐ | ☐ | | ☐ |
| Savings | ☐ | ☐ | | ☐ |
| Retirement Accounts | ☐ | ☐ | | ☐ |
| Business Interests and/or Ownership | ☐ | ☐ | | ☐ |
| Revocable Trust | ☐ | ☐ | | ☐ |
| Engagement Ring | ☐ | ☐ | | ☐ |
| Jointly Titled Premarital Assets | ☐ | ☐ | | ☐ |
| Other: | ☐ | ☐ | | ☐ |

# PRENUP PARTNERSHIP

| Premarital Debt | Separate | Marital | Custom Note | Seeking Attorney Guidance |
|---|---|---|---|---|
| Loans | ☐ | ☐ | | ☐ |
| Student Loans | ☐ | ☐ | | ☐ |
| Credit Card Balances | ☐ | ☐ | | ☐ |
| Payment Plans | ☐ | ☐ | | ☐ |
| Outstanding Obligations | ☐ | ☐ | | ☐ |
| Medical Debt | ☐ | ☐ | | ☐ |
| Jointly Titled Premarital Debt | ☐ | ☐ | | ☐ |
| Other: | ☐ | ☐ | | ☐ |

| Future Assets | Separate | Marital | Custom Note | Seeking Attorney Guidance |
|---|---|---|---|---|
| New Property | ☐ | ☐ | | ☐ |
| New Investments | ☐ | ☐ | | ☐ |
| Investment Appreciation | ☐ | ☐ | | ☐ |
| Retirement Savings Accumulated After Marriage | ☐ | ☐ | | ☐ |
| Income Earned After Marriage | ☐ | ☐ | | ☐ |
| Trust Income | ☐ | ☐ | | ☐ |

| | | | |
|---|---|---|---|
| Inheritance | ☐ | ☐ | ☐ |
| Business, Appreciation in Value | ☐ | ☐ | ☐ |
| Business, Created/ Acquired After Marriage | ☐ | ☐ | ☐ |
| Gifts Between Spouses | ☐ | ☐ | ☐ |
| Gifts from 3rd Parties | ☐ | ☐ | ☐ |
| Other: | ☐ | ☐ | ☐ |

| Future Debt | Separate | Marital | Custom Note | Seeking Attorney Guidance |
|---|---|---|---|---|
| New Loans | ☐ | ☐ | | ☐ |
| Increased Debt | ☐ | ☐ | | ☐ |
| New Credit Cards | ☐ | ☐ | | ☐ |
| Other: | ☐ | ☐ | | ☐ |

| Home | Separate | Marital | Custom Note | Seeking Attorney Guidance |
|---|---|---|---|---|
| Home Equity (already own) | ☐ | ☐ | | ☐ |
| Home Value Appreciation | ☐ | ☐ | | ☐ |
| Mortgage | ☐ | ☐ | | ☐ |
| New Home Purchase | ☐ | ☐ | | ☐ |
| Responsibility for Costs (e.g., maintenance, taxes, etc.) | ☐ | ☐ | | ☐ |
| Renovation Costs | ☐ | ☐ | | ☐ |
| Other: | ☐ | ☐ | | ☐ |

| Blended Family/ Estate Planning Considerations | N/A | Include Terms | Custom Note | Seeking Attorney Guidance |
|---|---|---|---|---|
| Responsibility for Expenses Related to Blended Family | ☐ | ☐ | | ☐ |
| Responsibility for Expenses Related to College | ☐ | ☐ | | ☐ |
| Bequests at Death | ☐ | ☐ | | ☐ |
| Life Insurance | ☐ | ☐ | | ☐ |
| Home - Terms Related to Treatment at First Death | ☐ | ☐ | | ☐ |
| Other: | ☐ | ☐ | | ☐ |

| Miscellaneous Terms | N/A | Include Terms | Custom Note | Seeking Attorney Guidance |
|---|---|---|---|---|
| Responsibility for Expense: _____ | ☐ | ☐ | | ☐ |
| Specify Responsibility or Process for Income Taxes | ☐ | ☐ | | ☐ |
| Spousal Support ("alimony" or "maintenance") | ☐ | ☐ | | ☐ |
| Attorney Fees | ☐ | ☐ | | ☐ |
| Pet Rights | ☐ | ☐ | | ☐ |
| Social Image | ☐ | ☐ | | ☐ |
| Sunset Clause | ☐ | ☐ | | ☐ |
| Gifting Requirement: _____ | ☐ | ☐ | | ☐ |
| Mediation and/or Arbitration | ☐ | ☐ | | ☐ |
| Fertility/Rights to Frozen Eggs | ☐ | ☐ | | ☐ |
| Other; | ☐ | ☐ | | ☐ |

| Behavior Incentives and Disincentives | N/A | Include Terms |
|---|---|---|
| Discuss with Your Attorney, if Applicable | ☐ | ☐ |

*If a particular behavior-related clause is permissible in your state, remember that enforcing these clauses often requires litigation.

# CHAPTER 13

# Including a Home in Your Prenup

*"Good buildings come from good people, and all problems*
*are solved by good design."*
—Stephen Gardiner

THE HOUSE is by far the most common source of conflict when it comes to prenup negotiations. This makes complete sense. A house is both a large investment—often the largest investment of an individual's life—and the shared family home where memories are made. It's often the most important item on a balance sheet, but it's also where we feel safest and where Santa brings gifts.

If you own a home, it's easily one of your biggest ongoing projects since you pour a tremendous amount of labor into the upkeep. The home is also a significant point of pride for many homeowners. It's financial and symbolic. I'm harping on this for good reason and so you don't take it lightly:

*The number one point of contention I run into is when one partner wants to look at the home purely from a financial perspective.*

That won't work, and that's because a house is often even more personal than money. And I hope by now it's becoming clear that money is deeply personal. As is the case with anything else you put in a prenup, the house requires each of you to sit with your wishes and fears and come up with a plan that truly feels good to both of you.

# CASE STUDY: INHERITING A FAMILY HOME

One couple, Alex and Samira, came to me with a creative formula for how they would split the equity in their home. They lived in Alex's family home but Samira was an independent young woman already earning a great income and really wanted to be able to build up equity in the home. Alex, being a real estate attorney, had come up with a detailed formula that he knew from a valuation standpoint was very generous.

Samira, an engineer, wasn't sure how to evaluate the formula. She clearly understood the formula but didn't know how she *felt* about it. I praised them for getting far enough along to come up with their own formula. I love that. But I also told them I wasn't surprised they were stuck, stating, "You wrote the formula before getting to the bottom of what you are solving for."

I could tell Samira had hesitations and she said something I hear often, "I just want to know that I'm going to be okay." No one wants to commit to a legal agreement that later leaves them feeling left in the lurch. But she didn't have much clarity about her needs or worries beyond that.

I gave them the homework assignment of going home and forgetting about the formula for now. Instead, I urged more conversations about . . .

- How do you plan to split other expenses apart from the home costs?

- What's important to each of you about your home? This house is important to Alex. Of course, it is. It's his family home. But this is becoming Samira's home, too.

- How will you address disagreements about decisions regarding the home? What if one of you wants to renovate the kitchen, and the other wants to save those funds for unrelated financial goals?

- Do you plan to have children? If so, would having children change your feelings about how much value you get out of the home versus maintaining the option to stay in the home with your children?

These types of discussions should happen over time and through many conversations. After talking and reflecting on what was said, you can come back to the formula and think about what would actually address both of your concerns.

Alex and Samira were excited by this assignment. They said they actually had already started to have talks about how to make the home theirs, so it would feel more like their family home, not just Alex's. I could tell they were already on the right track.

# CASE STUDY: PREMARITAL HOME EQUITY

Another couple I worked with also wanted help figuring out a fair way to treat their home in their prenup. Taylor had been married previously and was still raising three children in a home he owned. Karin had never been married before and didn't have children, but she was leaving her home country of Sweden to come make a life in the US with Taylor.

She knew if they were to divorce, she wouldn't care about staying in the home. She'd likely move back to Sweden. And Taylor wasn't necessarily determined to keep the home for his children, but he liked the idea of keeping that option. Karin did, however, strongly feel that she wanted their home to feel like their shared family home, not just Taylor's. Karin also didn't want to give up being close to her parents and extended family and end up with "nothing to show for it." She wanted to feel like her sacrifice was being honored.

Taylor had about $650,000 in equity built up in his home before they got married. Karin had funds from selling her home and planned to invest them in their home. A large amount of that would go toward upcoming renovations. I suggested they open a new joint account considered the "home" account. That's where they could deposit Karin's initial investment and deposit proportional amounts for ongoing costs beyond that.

Based on our conversations, I sent this couple three potential options for how they could split the value of their home in the prenup. I'll share these options with you as examples of just some of the ways you can divide the value of a home.

## Option 1: Split Proportional to Contributions

Under this option, the division of the parties' house value is based on the proportion of individual contributions.

In the case of Taylor and Karin, Taylor's estimated equity in the home at the time of marriage counts as his contribution. Based on an estimated home value of $1,210,000, Taylor's equity at the time of marriage was $650,000, while Karin is planning to invest $140,000. All told, the division would be as follows:

Taylor's Share: $650,000/($650,000 + $140,000) = 82%

Karin's Share: $140,000/($650,000 + $140,000) = 18%

**Suggestion:** Split all home expenses (after the $140,000 in funds contributed by Karin are used). According to these same percentages, they will follow this equation: Taylor: 82% and Karin: 18%.

## Option 2: Reimburse Original Contributions + Income-Based Split of Appreciation

In this option, each party is reimbursed for their original investments in the home prior to and early on in the marriage.

In Taylor and Karin's situation, this option treats Taylor's estimated equity in the home as his contribution. Any remaining appreciation in home value beyond that would be split proportional to their current salaries.

Taylor's Share: $650,000 + 67% of appreciation in value

Karin's Share: $140,000 + 33% of appreciation in value

**Suggestion:** Split all home expenses (after Karin's $140,000 in funds are used). According to these same percentages, the equation is Taylor: 67% and Karin: 33%.

## Option 3: Split Proportional to Contributions (without estimating current home value)

I created this option if this couple and subsequent clients did not like the idea of estimating a current home value (as in Options 1 and 2) to determine the value of Taylor's equity in the home.

In this option, you would tally Taylor's contributions toward the home to the best of your ability. This includes all mortgage payments, major repairs, and maintenance costs. I made up a hypothetical estimate of $425,000.

> **Note:** This option doesn't consider the amount of equity Taylor accumulated in the home *prior* to marriage.

Taylor's hypothetical total contribution = \$425,000

Taylor's Share: \$425,000/(\$425,000 + \$140,000) = 75%

Karin's Share: \$140,000/(\$425,000 + \$140,000) = 25%

**Suggestion:** Split all home expenses (after Karin's \$140,000 in funds are used). According to these same percentages, our new split is Taylor: 75% and Karin: 25%.

> **Note:** These options are suggestions and can be customized based on your preferences and mutual agreement. There are many ways you can go about dividing the value of a home in a prenup.

# THE MORTGAGE AND TITLE

You usually cannot add someone to a home mortgage without refinancing the mortgage. If one spouse will remain off the title, their credit will not benefit from the mortgage payments they're potentially contributing to. Keep this in mind during your discussions. Some people account for this by agreeing to make the non-mortgage-holding spouse the primary cardholder on a credit card for house expenses or general joint expenses.

The house title may be able to be updated to include the new spouse, even if the mortgage is just in one person's name. But some mortgage companies do require the title and mortgage to match, so you may need to check on this before making plans to change the title.

> **Note:** The title being in one name does not mean only that person gets the home or home equity in a divorce. If your prenup spelled out terms around this, those terms still apply. See the "Account Titles" section of Chapter 15: "Maintaining Your Agreement During Marriage" for more about titling and prenups.

# OPTIONS FOR YOUR HOME IN YOUR PRENUP

The home is one area where I see the most creative terms in prenuptial agreements. Here's a list of just some of the ways you can treat a home in a prenup.

## Leave It Out

If you don't include any terms regarding a home in your prenup and you go on to own a home *and* get divorced, your state laws will govern how you'll deal with your home and its value.

## Split the Value

You can agree in advance that you would split the value of the equity in your home 50/50, according to another proportion, or according to a formula.

## Protect Premarital Home Equity

If one partner owned the home before marriage, the prenup can state that the equity value they had amassed prior to marriage is protected as separate property, while any appreciation in value after marriage is still marital property. Or if one partner has already set aside designated premarital funds for a down payment on a first house, your prenup can spell out that the value of that contribution will be protected as separate property. This can also be a good option if those funds earmarked for a down payment are coming in the form of a family gift.

## Reimbursement for Contributions

You can set terms in your prenup to stipulate that any financial contributions to the improvement of the home above a certain value will be reimbursed to whoever made the contribution. For example, if one spouse pays $60,000 for a kitchen renovation, they would be reimbursed that $60,000 as part of any divorce settlement.

## Rights to Live in the Property

Your prenup can stipulate who would have the rights to continue living in your home if you split.

## Household Expenses

You can use your prenup to set provisions around who will be responsible for the household expenses. If one spouse is maintaining that a home is their separate property, it might be a good idea to additionally stipulate that that spouse is also responsible for the expenses of that house.

# CHAPTER 14

# Money and Couples Therapy

---

*"Learn from the mistakes of others. You can't live long
enough to make them all yourself."*
—Eleanor Roosevelt

IT'S NATURAL TO ASSUME that if you and your partner are dealing with a tense subject, a therapist is a smart place to go to gain insights into your situation.

That makes total sense.

You know what else makes total sense?

Therapists don't always get everything right.

Of course, I emphatically celebrate your interest in couples therapy! But use this chapter to sharpen your eye for what is and isn't working for you when it comes to money topics and couples therapy.

Regardless of what brings you to a therapist's office, you must be an active participant in sorting out what needs tending and what doesn't.

# GETTING HELP WITH THE CONVO

If you hit an impasse during the prenup process and are wondering, "Will couples therapy help us through it?" Or perhaps, if you simply love the idea of doing some proactive premarital counseling, I'd love to hear all about it. I refer my clients to therapy on a regular basis, whether they're getting a prenup or not. Individual and couples therapy has served me and my marriage well.

For relationships and tough money conversations, I'm particularly a fan of marriage and family therapists. I have found their training in relational dynamics to be especially helpful for couples. Hint: Look for therapists with MFT, LMFT, or LCMFT after their name. These stand for Marriage and Family Therapist, Licensed Marriage and Family Therapist, and Licensed Clinical Marriage and Family Therapist.

# OUR PERSONAL EXPERIENCE

My husband and I have worked with three different therapists. One was originally for premarital counseling; one we enlisted during a particularly difficult season of marriage, and the third we found more recently after I started a therapy skills course.

In the midst of making a leap to start my own practice and inspired by what I was learning in my Zoom therapy skills classes, I'd hop off the computer and go straight to my husband to tell him all about it. Soon, that turned into my saying, "Let's go back to therapy now that we're ready for the next level with these skills. I really think it will be powerful when we're not going out of desperation or resentment."

All three of these phases of therapy have been beneficial to us. This third phase really allowed us to go deep into the process—10/10: I highly recommend going before you're anxious for help.

Despite everything positive I have to say about what therapy has done for us, there are still areas where therapists bring in their own misgivings. We have to be responsible for helping sort out what is working in a healthy way and what needs work, particularly when it comes to money. We need to have the faith that we know what is best and be able to see clearly if the guidance we are being given makes sense for us.

Since the majority of my personal experience in this area is related to the wealth difference between my husband and myself, I'll share a bit about this topic first. Then, I'll share with you what I coach my prenup clients on before they go to therapy.

# WEALTH DIFFERENCE AND THERAPY

What is wealth difference? Like the phrase suggests, in this context, it just means one party has more wealth than the other. You'll usually hear the phrase "wealth disparity," but I don't love the word "disparity" as it pertains to a relationship, although I see this term used to relate to marriage and money frequently.

Indulge me for a minute . . . .

This seems as good a place as any to get on my soapbox for a minute and explain why I am a stickler about the use of this term. Disparity is usually referenced in situations that seem unfair or imply the gap should be closed, i.e., as represented in the phrases "economic disparities" or "age disparity." Yes, potential power dynamics are worthy of concern, but they shouldn't be applied to all relationships where one person came from family wealth and the other did not. I, for one, just want a healthy and strong partnership, no matter who brings what into the marriage.

Furthermore, if a wealth gap begs closing in a marriage, the way you would do that is by automatically assuming 100% of everything two partners own is completely shared, legally speaking. And that just doesn't make sense as a solution for everyone. See Chapter 7: "Do You Need a Prenup?"

# WHAT THERAPISTS TEND TO GET WRONG, IN MY EXPERIENCE:

- Therapists over-focus on the difference in wealth as a complication.
- They make assumptions about differences in wealth that might not apply.

Therapists fall into this habit because they are trained to be on high alert for power dynamics and abuse. Appropriately so!

*But we've had experiences with therapists who couldn't seem to stop peering through that particular lens, as if it was the most defining component of our relationship.*

I've heard similar feedback from an interracial couple and a cis-gender woman and a trans-woman couple. Of course, the differences between us are relevant in therapy; our lived experiences matter. But we also lose a lot of value in the process if everything is viewed through this "difference" lens.

This lens contributed to assumptions that my husband, who came from family wealth, was operating from a position of advantage over me instead of leaving some room to see where he needed support, too.

Not everything a couple struggles with should be viewed through the wealth-difference lens. It's also not easy to sort out what should and shouldn't be viewed through this lens. Just know that if you're in this situation, it's up to you to aid in the sorting-out process.

I'd venture to guess that if you have a life situation quite different from your therapist's (e.g., a different cultural background or gender identity), this will also create areas where you have to aid in disseminating what's relevant to your therapy and what's not.

The difference here is that we might share about our differing cultural backgrounds or gender identity experiences in many contexts, not just in therapy. These topics come up at school, work, and in our communities. However, therapy might be the first time and place you're participating in this sort of exercise around *money*. There's a novelty to the conversation and an uncertainty about how to talk about this subject since we don't regularly engage in conversations around it. Tensions can be higher as the topic itself is sensitive. I'm just asking you to be aware of these nuances.

Money was rarely the primary concern for my husband and me going into our therapy appointments. If it had been, that would have helped us dispel misconceptions faster.

One example of how this showed up was when a therapist suggested hiring out help as a solution to my complaint about carrying too much of the housework and childcare work. I'm all for hiring help—and I do—but I was seeking a stronger sense of partnership and shared responsibility with my husband. That therapist's suggestion wasn't the answer—it didn't touch what I was hoping for.

Our third therapist simply asked us directly (even though we hadn't brought it up), "How does your financial setup affect how you two operate? And how does your prenup affect your relationship?"

Elaborating on these answers gave us a chance to dispel his concern about our prenup and bring to light what was actually not working well—which in turn let us focus on the areas we really needed to, that were not rooted in a difference in wealth.

# PRENUPS AND COUPLES THERAPY

When I refer my prenup couples to therapy, I have to coach them first about how to approach this topic with their therapist. Let me share the same information with you so you can go into your sessions prepared with an understanding of where therapists are coming from if you happen to work with one who dislikes the idea of a prenup. Do not let your therapist talk you out of getting a prenup if it is important to you.

As a member of the Financial Therapy Association, I take skills courses alongside therapists from time to time, and I also do financial planning work for the Financial Therapy Clinical Institute.

I love therapists and the work they do. But I am seeing a commonality in how they view prenups. I've run into enough therapists who've outright rejected the idea that a prenup could be anything but harmful that I started asking them why. I was determined to understand the source of this strong belief. To date, every therapist I've asked has confirmed that therapists' training includes no discussion of prenups—which means they are potentially responding to their clients with their own bias.

But I digress.

If you're getting a prenup, you may need to educate your therapist a bit about how prenups can be used for good and not evil. Share your intentions for your prenup. Regardless of your therapist's feedback, I promise your reasons are valid and reasonable. Share this book if you have to!

Remember this mantra as you head into therapy to gain guidance in talking about your potential prenup: "Prenups are neutral tools. A prenup can make a marriage more equitable or less so—it's up to me."

If you're still running into outright resistance (I'd be a little surprised, honestly), please remember that therapy doesn't require blind faith. Therapy should feel helpful, not shameful. If your therapist isn't a great fit, keep searching.

That is my PSA regarding prenups and therapists. Please tell your friends.

# WHY DON'T THERAPISTS LIKE PRENUPS?

It would be easy to say that therapists' aversions to prenups come from the same places that create prenup stigma for many people. In some ways, that's true, but there's more to it than that.

*Therapists' training is highly focused on looking for power dynamics and anything that opens the door to abuse.*

Much like the rest of the population, many therapists mis-associate prenups with control and financial abuse.

This is honestly a reasonable conclusion if your only exposure to prenups is from movies and the media. Those prenups are exclusively about preventing a spouse from accessing funds or controlling a spouse's behavior. Yuck.

*The Brady Bunch didn't include any episodes about setting up a prenup to make sure Carol's family heirlooms got passed to Marcia, Jan, and Cindy instead of their stepdad, Mike.*

I'd love to see a movie about a billionaire who gets a prenup that includes annual vesting into his billions—an approach more generous than the default state laws that say he could simply keep it separate and never share it. But those aren't the movies getting made.

This impression that prenups are tools for control is also a reasonable conclusion if a therapist's only experience with them is in their office when a couple is fighting about one.

*Remember, as you are weighing your therapist's advice, that they mean well, but they are not trained in how prenups work.*

There's absolutely no reason that you should be discouraged from considering a prenup just because someone assumes it's a tool for abuse. You are the one who decides what's in your prenup. You decide what the terms are. You two, as a couple, agree on it. That's why it's an agreement. You don't have to set terms that create a situation of control or power imbalance. In fact, your prenup terms should do the opposite. It should protect both of you.

I want to also say that if you are in a relationship where you feel you are being manipulated or abused in any way, I hope you get out and protect yourself. What we are talking about in this book has nothing to do with nefarious motivations or abuse. Do not allow yourself to be coerced into a financially abusive relationship where you have lost control of your money. Manipulation is a huge red flag that you can't ignore.

# PREMARITAL COUNSELING

When my husband and I went to premarital counseling, I thought it would mean something to have an A+ from a professional. (A common theme of naïveté because I also thought we could just call up attorneys to start our prenup, and they'd tell us what to do. Please don't start the process that way, but back to my point . . . .)

Only you two are accountable for how this goes. Only you can gauge if marriage is the right step. How do you do that? My advice is to make sure you've talked about all the important topics I've brought up in this book, plus anything that's important to you personally (even if it's not on the traditional premarital topic lists).

Here's what I think is actually key . . . . Repeat. Those. Same. Convos.

Come back to those same topics over and over throughout the years. If you notice your feelings or beliefs around a subject have changed, bring it up. "Hey, I know we always said we would split work and expenses equally but this doesn't feel like I expected it would. Can we talk about it?"

*Some of the most surprising curveballs in marriage come when unspoken expectations finally find a voice.*

These are the assumptions that turn out to be false. I don't have a foolproof way to sniff out all of them, but the more you talk, the better, even if you think it's obvious you're in agreement.

Alright, now get out there and make your way together. You've got this.

# TIPS FOR SEARCHING FOR A THERAPIST

Working with these types of therapists helps you grow more at ease in talking about this critical topic. And remember, practice makes perfect! Now is the ideal time to set good money communication habits.

## Therapist Search Tips

- Search for therapists trained in couples work.
- Narrow your search using the below criteria.
- Interview therapists by phone or during an initial session.

## Therapists Databases

- American Association of Marriage and Family Therapy
- Financial Therapy Association
- Relational Life Therapy
- Emotionally Focused Couples Therapy (EFT)
- The Gottman Method Couples Therapy

## Look for Therapists Who . . .

- Have an advanced degree in the treatment of mental health, such as a master's degree or doctoral degree in the discipline of psychology, psychiatry, or social work. *I have a personal preference for marriage and family therapists who address repetitive relational dynamics.*
- Have experience and training working specifically with couples.
- Have licensure to practice in the state where you live.
- It's usually helpful to narrow your search by relevant topics, but you won't be able to filter a search for a therapist versed in prenups. *You will likely have to do some educating on the topic of prenups, no matter who you hire.*

*Most insurance will not cover couples therapy. Many great therapists may not accept insurance, either. If cost is a primary concern,

I suggest looking for a therapist who charges on a sliding scale. Alternatively, if your insurance covers couples therapy, look for a therapist who accepts your insurance. Great couples therapy and a great relationship will save you money long-term by avoiding divorce and financial problems borne out of miscommunication and misalignment.

## Questions to Ask:

- If you and your fiancé or fiancée only have certain times available for therapy, start by asking about therapists' availability.
- How and how much do you charge for sessions?
- Have you had formal supervised training in couples therapy?
- What are your views on prenuptial agreements and/or (insert primary area of concern)?
- Have you dealt with my issue before? Whether prenup-related or another primary concern.
- How do you structure your service, i.e., session length and frequency, and do you ever meet with just one partner?
- What treatment techniques do you use?
- What percentage of your clients are couples?
- What is a typical therapy timeline for the couples you see?

*There isn't necessarily a wrong answer to most of these questions. The goal is to look for responses that resonate with you.

# CHAPTER 15

# Maintaining Your Agreement During Marriage

---

*"There are no safe paths in this part of the world. Remember, you are over the Edge of the Wild now and in for all sorts of fun wherever you go."*
—J.R.R. Tolkien, The Hobbit

CONGRATULATIONS on making it this far in the book! I have wonderful news!

Creating an agreement you both feel great about was the hardest part. Whew! Maintaining your agreement is easy in comparison.

Let's now talk about implementing some concrete rules for maintaining your agreement as well as some best practices for responsible prenup-havers.

## THE DOCUMENT

You'll likely sign two original prenuptial agreements when all is said and done. You and your partner will each get to keep one original. Be sure to get an electronic copy as well. The electronic copy will come in handy when you inevitably make updates to your estate plans in the future.

Keep your prenup somewhere safe. You might even ask your attorney to prepare three originals so that you and your partner can each keep one in private locations, and you can keep a third in a secure location you will both agree on and share.

> **Note:** Don't leave the original with your attorney. Attorneys only have to hold onto documents for so long.

# ACCOUNT TITLES

Ask your attorney for guidance on account and property titles if you have any questions about how your assets should be titled to fit your prenup. Generally, if you have separate property, it should remain in your individual name. Anything considered marital property under your prenup can be titled in individual name or joint name—it's still marital property as long as it's identified as such.

*Now, this part is important: If the separate property is in joint name, it is no longer separate, no matter what your prenup says.*

If you bought your house before you got married and your prenup says it's your separate property if you split, but you change the title to reflect a joint name, you've likely thrown that protection out the window. There are some caveats to that, but don't play around in caveat land. Play it safe, and don't put separate property in joint name. As with everything else, listen to your attorney's advice first and foremost.

# TRANSFERS

In addition to account title mistakes, transfers are another way people accidentally commingle their separate and marital property. To avoid this, don't transfer separate property money into accounts with marital property money or vice versa.

If you have automatic transfers or deposits set up for premarital accounts, you might need to change those instructions before getting married. For example, if your premarital savings will remain separate property, but you currently have your paychecks deposited to the account that holds those savings, you will want to direct your paychecks to a new account going forward.

# IMPORTANT REMINDERS!

## The IRS Doesn't Care What's in Your Prenup

Your prenup can define who is responsible for particular percentages of your joint taxes, but it's still a joint tax return to the IRS. You're both still responsible for the taxes. If your partner doesn't hold up their end of the agreement stipulating that they are to pay 100% of the taxes, your avenue for recourse is to take your spouse to court. Don't expect that you can show your prenup to an IRS agent to get out of your obligation to pay taxes.

## The Bank Doesn't Care What's in Your Prenup, Either

Your prenup can denote that an individual account is marital property, but that doesn't mean the bank will let you make a withdrawal from an account that's only in your spouse's name. Financial institutions can only follow the titling of an account or a court order. It's up to you and your partner to set up your account to reflect your agreement correctly.

*While I'm happy to see the stigma of prenups melting away, please remember it's not an all-powerful document that fixes all problems.*

Ultimately, it's up to you and your spouse or partner to follow the rules of your prenup. If your spouse breaks the rules, your options are to 1) let it go, 2) hand your spouse a strongly worded letter, 3) take your spouse to court, or, if you get divorced, 4) resolve it as part of your divorce agreement. Regarding option #3, I personally haven't heard of anyone taking their spouse to court while also intending to stay married. It's hard to imagine anyone choosing that avenue, but it's an option you can take, nonetheless.

# ACCOUNTING

Save the month-end and year-end statements for all your accounts, assets, and debts when you get married. Financial institutions will only keep these available for a certain period of time. Banks are required to keep statements for 5-7 years. Certain account types, say for a completed auto loan, may be available for as little as 12 months. So, it's important to save your own copies.

# INHERITANCES AND GIFTS

Inheritances generally maintain special protections if you keep them separate from your marital property. This is usually the case whether you have a prenup or not. Some states also have protections for gifts. Unless you've consulted an attorney in your state and know this to be true, don't mix your inheritance with gift money! If this is an area where you want concrete clarity, consider putting a clause in your prenup to address inheritances and gifts.

# ONGOING TRANSPARENCY

Make a plan for ongoing transparency. Use an online tool to share account balances and agree to bring up any new financial undertakings. Decide on ground rules concerning when you can make decisions independently versus separately. Lots of couples set a purchase limit –a specific dollar amount that necessitates they agree to discuss the purchase decision together.

# BOUNDARIES

Similar to your ground rules around transparency and spending, include ground rules for financial boundaries. By creating a prenup, you're already creating boundaries within your marriage, but what about financial boundaries between you and the rest of the world? Who are you comfortable sharing financial information with? Will you consult family when making large financial decisions?

Set a general rule, deciding whether you want to be open to helping friends and family financially when needed, for instance. Is there an amount above which you should discuss these decisions together? Have you thought about if you are comfortable accepting financial help from family should that need arise? Just like many of the topics here, this should be an ongoing conversation.

# REVIEW AND REVISE

Set regular intervals to review your big-picture finances, e.g., annually at the same time of year. Commit to a habit like this early on, and you'll have an easier time adjusting your financial setup as your lives change.

With regard to your prenup specifically, you can always amend it if you find that some terms no longer fit your life situation.

In case you are wondering, *does amending my prenup make it a postnup?* That depends on your state. In some states, you can amend your prenup during your marriage, and it will still be considered a prenuptial agreement in the eyes of the law. In other states, when you amend your prenup, you're converting it into a postnuptial agreement. In either case, the option is available to make amendments to best represent your changing needs.

# PROFESSIONAL SERVICES

Tell your accountant, financial advisor, and all your relevant professional service providers that you have a prenup, and share with them the terms they need to know about. Advise your CPA, for example, that you are responsible for the taxes resulting from your separate property business and that you need help calculating your portion of what is due.

If you have a life insurance requirement in your prenup, tell your insurance rep the required coverage amount and ask them to alert you before any term policy lapses.

*And please, for the love of all things, tell your estate planning attorney that you have a prenup.*

I cannot tell you how many people I've encountered who had estate plans drawn up without considering their prenup terms. Your estate plan needs to be drafted to fit the terms of your prenup.

Don't forget, your prenup is your responsibility to uphold. Take good care of it and review it periodically.

# THE NEWLYWED CHECKLIST

## Sample Newlywed Finances Checklist

| Bank and Investment Accounts | Partner 1 | Partner 2 | Custom Note |
|---|---|---|---|
| Open new, post-marital individual bank accounts and investment accounts. This helps keep your premarital assets separate. | ☐ | ☐ | |
| Save the statements of any of your premarital assets so you have a record of their values at the time of marriage. | ☐ | ☐ | |
| Open new joint account(s), if applicable. | ☐ | ☐ | |
| Update direct deposit instructions, if applicable. | ☐ | ☐ | |
| Update bill payment instructions, if applicable. | ☐ | ☐ | |

| | | | |
|---|---|---|---|
| Update beneficiary designations on 401k and other retirement accounts. | ☐ | ☐ | |
| Other: | ☐ | ☐ | |

| Tax | Partner 1 | Partner 2 | Custom Note |
|---|---|---|---|
| Confirm if you should file taxes jointly. *Include details of any income-based student loan repayment program or other income-based benefits you count on.* | ☐ | ☐ | |
| Update tax withholding with your employer. | ☐ | ☐ | |
| If your name changed, make sure it's also updated with the Social Security Administration *before* filing your next tax return. | ☐ | ☐ | |
| If either of you make estimated tax payments quarterly, update your estimated amounts due according to your new joint estimates. | ☐ | ☐ | |
| Other: | ☐ | ☐ | |

| Insurance and Estate Planning | Partner 1 | Partner 2 | Custom Note |
|---|---|---|---|
| Compare employer health plans and decide if you should go on one plan or stay on separate plans. (If you were already on the same health plan, update the plan with your new marital status.) | ☐ | ☐ | |
| Update (or get) wills and healthcare POAs. | ☐ | ☐ | |
| Review life insurance coverage amounts | ☐ | ☐ | |
| Update life insurance beneficiary designations. | ☐ | ☐ | |
| Do the two of you own vehicles? Review your auto insurance policies to take advantage of cost savings from consolidating, if possible | ☐ | ☐ | |

| Do you need to update homeowners or renters insurance? In light of the combined value of your belongings (including jewelry), you could add your spouse to your policy and update your coverage, or vice-versa. | ☐ | ☐ | |
| Other: | ☐ | ☐ | |

| Prenup | Partner 1 | Partner 2 | Custom Note |
| --- | --- | --- | --- |
| Review prenup terms. | ☐ | ☐ | |
| Confirm your accounts, account titles, direct deposits, and bill payments are set up correctly to fit any relevant terms of your prenup. | ☐ | ☐ | |
| Start a habit of checking in annually to make sure your estate plans, prenup, and financial setup all still feel right for your life situation. Any of these can be amended, if needed. | ☐ | ☐ | |
| Other: | ☐ | ☐ | |

| Other | Partner 1 | Partner 2 | Custom Note |
|---|---|---|---|
| Cancel duplicate subscriptions. | ☐ | ☐ | |
| Set up a password vault for sharing logins and passwords. | ☐ | ☐ | |
| Other: | ☐ | ☐ | |

# CHAPTER 16

# Prenup FAQs

---

*"We went to dinner, and my fiancé's mother brought out an actual prenup drafted by her lawyer. She put it in front of me after dinner and told me to sign. Obviously, I didn't read it, let alone sign it."*
—One sad Redditor teaching us what not to do

I THINK OF THIS FINAL CHAPTER as a place you can return to again and again to get a refresher on the answers you need to know as you are building your prenup.

In the following pages, I'm sharing some of the most common questions I hear from clients to let you know you're not alone (this process is confusing and overwhelming to many) so you can antici-pate the answers you may need.

Let's get to it!

# COMMON QUESTIONS

## How Long Does It Take to Get a Prenup?

I recommend beginning your prenup prep process at least six months before your wedding date. This allows enough time to start with a financial plan first.

Even better, embark on it as soon as you're engaged. The more time you have, the less rushed you will feel and the less pressure there will be on these really important conversations.

Also, make sure you allow time for an attorney search and interviews.

If you're under a tight timeline (three months or less), make sure that's the first thing you communicate to your attorney.

## How Often Do Prenups Fail?

Most prenups never see the light of day after they are signed, so we don't have a good way of measuring how often they fail. Prenups that get challenged in court generally hold up at the same rates as wills and trusts. The idea that they're frequently thrown out is completely wrong.

## Are Prenups Always Private?

You may choose to file a prenup with the courts for recording purposes, but otherwise, prenups are private agreements. If a prenup ends up being challenged in court, it will become part of the court record. Similarly, if a divorce is contested in court, it will also become part of public record.

# Will a Prenup Ensure an Easy Divorce?

Divorce is a painful process. I would never want to lead someone to believe a prenup would make it easy. Divorce sucks. But a good prenup can make the divorce process simpler, faster, and less expensive. Ideally, if you end up needing to use your prenup, it will govern the bulk of the big decisions in front of you and leave very little remaining to be sorted out.

# Can I Use a Trust Instead of Getting a Prenup?

The simplest way for me to answer that question is to explain the difference between a prenup and a trust. Then, you can see the benefits and other considerations laid out for you and decide which is the right fit. I'll run down prenup advantages here once more and contrast them with the trust option. You get to decide what works for you based on your goal.

## Prenup:

- Transparency/open communication
- Protects future assets, retirement plan(s)
- Protection from debt
- Sets obligations during the marriage
- Requires a couple to plan for the future
- Can set rules for future hypotheticals

## Trust:

- May be able to remain hidden
- Less risk of commingling
- Family can maintain control

- Can be set up unilaterally
- Ongoing admin work, tax filings, etc.
- Can only address assets that already exist

It's also important to note that only certain types of trusts would be treated as separate property without a prenup, and some states will still treat income from those trusts as marital property or as a source of income factored into a spousal support calculation.[17,18]*

If, after everything you've read and researched, you still find yourself facing specific challenges, there is hope.

I am dedicating this next section to the people who call and message me saying . . . .

# HELP! WHAT IF ...

Here are my answers to many of the SOS calls and messages I receive:

## What if my fiancé is immigrating to the US?

Prenups have additional enforceability considerations when immigration is involved, so be sure to hire an attorney with experience preparing prenups for US citizens and immigrant spouses. *The Generous Prenup* by Laurie Israel—Chapter 13, in particular—is a great source for information about how the requirements of the United States Citizenship and Immigration Services (USCIS) and the requirements of an enforceable prenup interact.

---

17    Friedman, Pam. *I now pronounce you financially fit: How to protect your money in marriage and divorce.* Austin: River Grove Books, 2015, p. 86).

18    *The aforementioned book* was my source for this info, although I generally already knew it.

I also highly recommend listening to the *Emotional Investment* podcast series by financial therapist Amanda Clayman on Audible. She has recorded sessions with two different couples, including a fiancé immigrating to the US and one couple even considering a prenup during their session.

## What if my partner's attorney drafted a prenup without my input?

It's never too late to pause the prenup process and regroup to do it right.

If you've been handed a prenuptial agreement and you're over-whelmed, pause. Sit down with your partner and talk through what you two actually want this agreement to do before you go back to coordinating with your attorneys. This will save you a lot of stress and money.

Remember, you can make an agreement that you both feel great about and protects everyone.

If you need help regrouping and reaching a mutual understanding about your prenup, contact me at www.kaylindillon.com.

## What if family is involved in our prenup?

If you are comfortable seeking advice from your parents, that's great. What matters most is that you and your partner are both comfortable with the level of input you allow each of your families to have in the prenup process. And, ultimately, make sure whatever you agree to is what *you* want.

## What if I feel pressured?

Do not sign something out of pressure. It will hang over your marriage. During coaching sessions with individuals feeling pressured, I remind them, "Future you is counting on you to look out for yourself." If you're in this situation, make sure you've hired a professional who will put you first.

## What if we still can't agree?

Reach out to professionals for help if you still can't agree, and obviously, don't sign the prenup. You're better off getting married with state laws you don't love than with a legal agreement that makes you uncomfortable.

Let me also give you this bit of wisdom shared with me by L. Paul Hood, Jr. "If you try to win every point, you're going to lose the war. It's going to be a pyrrhic victory at best."

## What if I already signed an agreement I don't love?

Speak up about your feelings. Then, amend it! If you're not ready to do that, start by addressing the underlying factors in your relationship that led you to this point. When did you realize you don't love the agreement? What isn't sitting right with you? I highly recommend couples therapy to help you sort it out and give a little more volume to your voice. Your feelings are important, so advocate for yourself and speak up!

## What if I'm already married?

You can get a postnuptial agreement if you're already married. A lot of the concepts here about how to prepare for that process would apply. There's a bit more variation in rules regarding postnups from state to state, so hire a family law attorney or an estate planning attorney licensed in your state to help you with this.

## What if we don't plan to marry?

If you aren't married and don't have plans to get married but do plan to join your finances in some fashion, you can get a cohabitation agreement. This is especially important if you are, say, buying a house together. Follow the same prep process outlined in this book and hire a family law attorney to help you draft the agreement.

# MY THREE BEST TIPS

As you embark on the prenup-getting journey, let me leave you with this:

1. Learn about prenuptial agreements together.

   *It's your job to be prepared and to make an agreement that supports the relationship you want. It's your attorney's job to advise you on your individual best interests, financially speaking.*

2. Discuss your goals for your prenup before starting the drafting process with an attorney.

   *Identify separate and marital property, premarital and post-marital assets, and specify plans for your home.*

3. Hire a divorce attorney.

   *Divorce attorneys work in the closest proximity to prenup case law. Ask how they charge, how many prenups they've done, and if they have experience with a prenup being tested in court. A "yes" to that last question is ideal, but it doesn't give you a failsafe that this will be your outcome. Do the work to give your prenup the best shot at protecting your individual and joint interests.*

Regardless of your future outcome, I wish you the best. You have taken the first step to prepare yourself for establishing a solid and protective prenup that can benefit you and your partner and, when conceived with compassion, may even deepen your relationship. That's a goal worth reaching for and having tough conversations for. It's a goal that can give your marriage more fuel to go the long haul. Use it as a tool to help you accomplish that throughout your many fulfilling years.

Here's to loving love and safeguarding it completely the way you both deserve.

Thank you for investing your time in reading this book. If you would like more information about getting started on your prenup or need additional clarity around the process, please visit www.kaylindillon.com. I'd be delighted to connect with you.

# ACKNOWLEDGMENTS

THANK YOU to all the couples and individuals who lent their time and shared their stories with me for my book research. I still carry your experiences with me, and I'm not finished putting your shared lessons to use.

Thank you to my clients who trusted me and engaged in the pre-nup prep process with dedication and openness. Your stories and experiences have enriched this book in immeasurable ways. I'm grateful for the opportunity to work with you and to witness the clarity and confidence that emerged from our sessions together.

I also want to thank Nathan Astle and Edward Coambs for teaching me skills I use with my couples every day. I value you both highly as colleagues and dear friends.

Thank you to my in-laws, who have only ever supported me. A daughter-in-law talking publicly about her prenuptial agreement is not exactly comfortable, but only your encouragement has shown through to me. Your faith in my work and willingness to stand by me means the world to me.

Thank you to L. Paul Hood, Jr. for the invaluable knowledge and encouragement.

Many, many thanks to my editor and publisher, Hilary Jastram, and her team at Bookmark Publishing House. In more ways than I could ever say, I couldn't have done this without Hilary.

Thank you to Cheryl Denton for being a trusted advocate and teacher many years ago. You helped plant a seed that continues to influence the work I do today.

# ABOUT THE AUTHOR

KAYLIN DILLON is a financial planner with expertise in prenuptial agreements. A passionate advocate for making money matters transparent and accessible, she started her career in 2012 at Morgan Stanley as a Financial Advisor and Portfolio Manager.

Driven by her desire to modernize financial planning for couples with prenups and engaged lovebirds contemplating their financial future together, Kaylin founded Kaylin Dillon Financial Planning in 2021. Her dedication to this unique niche has earned her recognition in respected publications such as *CNN, Bloomberg, Investment News, NerdWallet, The Wall Street Journal, and Financial Planning* magazine.

Kaylin is on a mission to make prenup-getting less daunting for engaged couples. To further the cause, she established The Prenup Coach®—a platform where she provides invaluable knowledge and support to couples at all stages of the prenuptial agreement process.

Kaylin has been married with a prenup since 2010. She and her husband live in Lawrence, Kansas, with their daughter. Please visit www.kaylindillon.com to learn more and connect with her.

# DISCLOSURES

THE CONTENT OF THIS BOOK is intended purely for general educational purposes and should not be construed as investment, financial planning, tax, legal, or other professional advice. Any recommendations, templates, guides, or other resources have been included solely to serve as the starting point for readers to adapt and customize based on their personal situation. Though the author may be an investment adviser representative and owner of Kaylin Dillon Financial Planning, LLC, a registered investment adviser, specifically tailored investment or financial planning advice may only be rendered separately pursuant to the signing of a written agreement.

The author and publisher have made every effort to include the most updated and accurate information in this book and are not liable or responsible for any discrepancies or financial, tax, legal, investment, professional, or any other results the reader may or may not experience from the application of the book's content.

The content of this book has been drawn from a composite of client cases. All identifying personal and factual information has been changed. Any resemblance to a particular couple's situation or individual's situation is coincidental.

www.ingramcontent.com/pod-product-compliance
Lightning Source LLC
Chambersburg PA
CBHW071951260326
41914CB00004B/796